A
Hidden
Life

Also by Johanna Reiss

The Upstairs Room
The Journey Back

A Hidden Life

A Memoir of August 1969

Johanna Reiss

 **MELVILLE**HOUSE
BROOKLYN, NEW YORK

Melville House Publishing
145 Plymouth Street
Brooklyn, New York 11201

mhpbooks.com

First Melville House Printing: January 2009

ISBN: 9781933633558

Library of Congress Cataloging-in-Publication Data

Reiss, Johanna.
   A hidden life : a memoir of August 1969 / by Johanna Reiss.
      p. cm.
   ISBN 978-1-933633-55-8
   1. Reiss, Johanna. 2. Reiss, Johanna--Travel--Netherlands. 3. Jews-
-Netherlands--Biography. 4. Hidden children (Holocaust)--Nether-
lands--Biography. 5. Bereavement--Personal narratives. 6. Jews,
Dutch--New York (State)--New York--Biography. 7. Netherlands--
Biography. I. Title.
   DS135.N6R439 2008
   940.53'18092--dc22
     [B]
                                       2008007087

With wobbly steps I walked over to my window. It was covered with a layer of ice. I opened my mouth wide and breathed on it. Slowly the ice melted. I stopped when enough of the window was clear to let me see outside. Sky.

—from *The Upstairs Room*

DURING WORLD WAR II, as a Jewish child, I was hidden with my sister Sini by the Oostervelds, a family of Dutch farmers. The hamlet was Usselo, so small it is easy to pass through and not know you have done so.

A decade after the war was over—of course, there'll never be another one, we snapped at the time, not after this one—I came to the United States, for one year supposedly. It stretched out to many more. I married an American, Jim, also a Jew, although barely, a box of matzos at Passover time, that was it.

It was his idea that I write about my time in hiding: two years, seven months, and part of one more day. "Write about what it was like, how you and your sister survived. Our children are old enough to understand at least some of it. Tell them how those people, who didn't know you, or Sini, took you in."

Together with my daughters Kathy and Julie, who were still very young, I went to Holland in July of 1969 to steep myself in the war I had lived through. It was going to be a long trip, seven weeks, but well worth it. It would take time to find what I had pushed way down, to haul it closer. And unwrap it. I needed to be back in that room. I needed to sit on the same chair again, close my eyes, and search for the child I had been "then."

The result became *The Upstairs Room,* a story that starts when war had just broken out and almost no one realized what was going on. We had heard that Hitler hated Jews. Not the Dutch ones, we said, blinded.

Invasion. Occupation. Stern warnings. This was forbidden, then that. Until life was reduced to waiting for transportation, east, always east. In trains that left on a Tuesday and exactly on schedule, the hour before dawn.

If only we could find someone to take care of us, to help us, keep us, give us a chance at least.

It was safer and potentially easier to find a willing host if we split up. My father went one way, my older sister, Rachel, another, but not until, from behind a brave shopkeeper's window, she saw the hearse go by holding our mother, who had been sick in the hospital and had died just before the soldiers would have taken her away. Only then, when there was nothing Rachel could do for mother anymore did she leave Winterswijk, our hometown, to go to her place of shelter, the last Jew still skulking around. Sini and I had found refuge with the Oostervelds: Johan, his wife Dientje, and his mother, whom we, like everyone else in Usselo, called Opoe. They were poor, uneducated. No running water, an outhouse.

We stayed upstairs, one endless day after another, hoping there'd be a next one to be endless and that one day we could see the world from outside again.

Sometime during that summer of 1969, in the middle of our trip, Jim came to Holland. He saw where I had been hidden, met the people who had sheltered me, walked around the tiny room my sister Sini and I had shared. He returned to New York ahead of the children and me. Seven days later he killed himself. He was thirty-seven. There was no note.

It took many years before I was able to write about my childhood. It has taken many more before I had the courage to tell this story, of trying to understand the mystery of Jim's death.

I was in Winterswijk, my hometown, when the phone call came. It was August 24th, 1969.

Part I

THE WAR that was never going to be followed by another one had been over for almost twenty-five years. In many parts of the world, plans were being made to commemorate the event, a speech here, a parade there, and "It Shall Never Happen Again" in places in between.

In New York, protests against the war in Vietman bounced off buildings and some people burned themselves alive, an act, said Jim, that showed how deeply they felt about the war. Not so, I said in the safety of my living room: "They're using the cause: They're sick."

In Holland, as an early anniversary present, the Dutch minister of justice suggested the release of the last three war criminals still in jail. "Why keep them any longer?" he said. "It's costly, inhuman, they're old, no longer well. Let's send them back."

"Don't!" people who had gathered in The Hague, the seat of government, screamed. Sini screamed too, and fainted. She said so in a letter that I read in my living room in New York. "Don't ... remember what happened with the one that was let go because of some incurable disease the doctor said he had? Once across the German border he all but strutted out of the ambulance and was given a hero's welcome."

Had I already been in Holland I wouldn't have taken to the streets, nor joined in the shouting. Encouraged too much by Johan, the man in whose house, room, bed I was saved: "Annie"—my nickname as a kid—"gives you no trouble, a good thing, too. I'll tell you why, I don't know exactly the, what-d'you call-'m, ins and outs, but some Jew had to be shot by the people who took'm in. He always wanted something, and complained if it didn't come quickly enough. They couldn't take it any more."

1969 had been a year of unrest everywhere. Holland too had protesters against the war in Southeast Asia. Those born after the Americans did their liberating paraded about, buttons on denim shirts and in outfits their parents had discarded as soon as stores carried wearables again. Wrong is wrong; buttons and throats yelled "Yankee Go Home!" It was also the year in which tour buses, shiny and bearing names like *Reiselust* and *Lebensfreude*, fanned onto Dutch roads. Buses filled with middle-aged Germans, men in stiff blue caps, loudly pointing out *guck mal*—"look"—where they had done their fighting.

These same roads were also crowded with caravans, filled with Dutch people dressed meticulously in something the Americans had invented: clothing that wouldn't wrinkle, no matter how long you'd sit in it. And sit they would, all the way to Normandy, to the cemeteries where Allied soldiers lay buried. *Requiem aeternam dona eis, Domine.* Sure, it was not a cheery thing to be doing for their vacations, but this was a special occasion, exactly twenty-five years after D-day. Just think, all those young men who had been told to cross the ocean—a lot of them surely had not wanted to—and face the enemy so Europe could be free again. With them they carried candles and jars to put flowers in, once they got there.

I know, my own trip, I keep pushing it away—I'm getting there.

THE FLIGHT TO AMSTERDAM had been good. It left on time, our daughters had not thrown up as they had threatened. Everything was fine. I woke them up. "Come, *girletjes*," already adding a diminutive—very Dutch. "Come *snoetjes*, we'll be there soon."

Yes, Daddy would come and see us. They knew but asked anyway. "In just nineteen days, don't you worry."

Smiling into the plane window, it dawned on me again that it was going to be Jim's first visit to Holland. It would have been such a long separation otherwise, we said. Was he still in the office? Or was I all wrong about the time difference again and was he just waking up, getting ready, polishing his shoes past the point where they already shone like mirrors? Or doing his exercises? Stationary runs culminating in half a dozen scissor jumps. He'd better be careful with those, not land on his ankle again as he did last year: He couldn't walk for a week.

The plane descended some more. With my arms around Kathy and Julie I waited for Holland to become real, those squares of green and yellow, the red-tiled roofs, and cows that didn't look up no matter how low the plane flew.

Already, down below, the North Sea flowed. Soon I'd see it in Scheveningen, the beach resort of The Hague where Sini had been living for a long time now. Where donkeys, I told Kathy and Julie, wait along the water's edge offering rides. Sure, to them too. Why not? Could that tiny speck be interpreted as a boat? Fishing for herring perhaps? Jim would love them.

My kids asked about their father again. Yes, still in nineteen days. Did they think we had been flying for a week? Which set me thinking of time again, how little left, how much more to go ....

It had been three years since I had last been to Holland, by myself then. Father had died, and all the way from Schiphol Airport to Winterswijk, in a limo courtesy of my stepsister, I saw that trees were changing color. I had forgotten that trees do that in Holland too. I didn't know exactly what had happened to Father, in his car, yes, on his way to a cattle market, I'd heard. I had rushed over from New York once before when he'd had an accident.

"Stop driving," Mr. de Leeuw, the doctor, told him then, "You don't seem to be able to control yourself." My stepmother had been in the car too that time. In a thick fur coat, she barely got a scratch.

Strange, there would be no Father at the airport this time, telling me to relax, that I looked tired, why not close my eyes, he'd get us there, but already speeding and jiggling the steering wheel as he tried to figure out whether to go left, right, or continue straight ahead.

My sisters would be waiting. Still, Rachel drove a little like Father, as if she too were a cattle dealer, chasing after cows with high milk yield and fat content, papers to prove it. And cheap.

"Do you remember your Opa?" I asked my kids. "And how!"

"Cookies and visits to farmers," they shrieked with one voice. I tightened my arms around them.

When they had got into the car with him, they'd wave at me too, trustingly, "Bye Mommy." He'd go slowly with them, he promised, he knew the roads, every curve, stone, pebble and whatnot. If something had happened after all ... why had I not said no to him?

I didn't know it, but he carried a picture of Kathy and Julie in his car. I dislodged it from the glove compartment in the garage where the wreck had been towed, my stepmother couldn't do it. That's when I cried, that my children were so important to him but he almost never had a chance to see them.

I didn't arrive with thoughts of death. I really didn't. The second we landed I noticed the sky was blue, it was warm too, all wrong. In the country of my childhood it rained, drizzled at least. I had packed almost nothing for warm dry weather.

"Move your feet, *poesjes*," in Dutch now. I pulled them along. They were poking each other already. Quick, over to the luggage. You could see the street from there.

So many faces. Which ones? Yes, yes, yes, there. I saw them.

Sini rolled up a sleeve. My arms were tanned too, many hours on the terrace. Rachel was tapping her watch. I knew she wanted coffee, wanted it now.

I pointed to my kids and mouthed: "Grown, right?" Sure, seven and nine already. I ran back to the conveyor belt, collected suitcases and children, and pushed everything in the direction of the glass door.

"What do we say, Mom?"

"Who cares?" I yelled. They should have listened when I tried to teach them Dutch. "Say anything. Don't bother me now."

"Sini!" I shouted. My lips trembled. "Rachel!"

"Annie!" I heard.

Here we were, three sisters, all of us having defied the enemy's plan. That's how I began my summer, celebrating life.

THE WEATHER STAYED BEAUTIFUL. That too marked my visit. What have we got on our hands, people marveled. In Spain of course, they get these temperatures, in Greece and Italy sure, but here? Makes you look at your own country in a different way. There was a shortage of ice cream, an abundance of fleas and furs draped over store mannequins with sunglasses.

Bicyclists go slowly, papers warned, after one overcome by heat, fell into a canal and drowned.

Each morning, the sky already trembling with heat, my kids and I left Sini's apartment and walked over to the sea, a very short distance, across one street, a few steps farther, and there it was, water shimmering. I'd follow them down concrete steps and onto the boardwalk, crowded even at this early hour. We walked past dogs and people, skirts tucked, pantlegs rolled, already dipping into bags of French fries topped with mayonnaise, as in Belgium, a barrel organ sending forth odes, *To the Old Canal*. A group of teens doing the same for Jesus.

Every few meters, wooden steps led down to cafés erected on the sand for the summer.

We'd drop Sini off at her favorite one, "the Seahorse," where other survivors tended to come and talk about anything but "then"—the war. One regular, Judith, had let slip, Sini said, that she was relieved when she got caught; at least the tension of "When will it be?" was over. Hiding had been humiliating, and in camp she was not alone; there she had been with "her own people."

Better run after my kids then, quick, before they reached the water. "Not above the knees, you hear?"

I stayed where I could see them, close by. In fifteen days Jim would be here, same spot. He'd jump in, joyfully, and swim, a kid clutching to his neck. "Great, Mom," they'd say, once back on the sand, "but scary." He'd want to carry me in next.

"Come, Ann, your turn."

No, I'd answer, one big smile, some other time maybe.

My kids were fine, jumping up and down in barely a wave. Overhead, in spite of no wind, a few kites, and a little plane lazily pulling along a message: "Use Condoms, Prevent the Misery of Adam and Eve." From behind, sounds drifted over, a shred of music, guitar, drum, a phonograph? Someone singing:

> *Everybody's talking at me. I don't hear a word*
> *they're saying. Only the echoes of my mind.*

I thought of Shelter Island, a train and ferry ride away from Manhattan where we had gone on vacation the year before, to a cottage right on the bay. I had been frightened, especially after Kathy and Julie had gone to bed, and I sat at the table thinking about writing about my time in hiding, only not admitting it yet. I had been just as frightened on weekends, when Jim came. Not in the afternoon, when he glided through the water in a kayak, looking so handsome, thin and muscular. I was afraid late at night when he'd take a swim. Where was he, I couldn't see him, I could barely hear splashing. He's a good swimmer, I'd tell myself, he grew up near water, the Delaware River, where he swam off the dam when he was what, eight? Where was he now, though, all I could see was darkness, intensified by an eerie stillness. It was the same terror I felt after my father remarried and he and my stepmother went out one evening and I heard, saw, trees and bushes creep forward, like soldiers combing an area. Or had it not been right after the war, but in the beginning, Father already in hiding, the first Jew in Winterswijk to have done so. Mother was in the hospital. And Rachel and Sini were out after curfew when they shouldn't have been out—Decree 198, Article One—carrying our belongings to neighbors who were willing to store them for us, so that in case we lived through it all we'd have something to start with. And I wasn't allowed to come. I might stumble again—like the one time they gave in and I fell against a basket of dishes. At least it had been a sound, something to have broken the stillness.

The song was over. My kids were still splashing and shrieking. I never understood that kind of fun. The same with skating. Or being on a dance floor where my legs seemed like vanes pushing against the wind.

I looked up at the sky. A new kite had been added, its

long tail swinging back and forth like the pendulum of a clock, badly out of step.

I called my kids over. "Let's see what Tante Sini is up to." They had just filled their pails for a sand castle—*slosh, slosh*—which, once Jim arrived, he promised, would turn into an edifice with windows and drawbridges and a roadway down which they could roll a ball, which ultimately would plop into a pool of water. His father had made something like that for him when he was very little and they vacationed on Cape May, before his parents divorced.

I needed to ask Sini more about the war, ours and beyond, about her ex-husband's war, and about her new friend's. Questions I'd never ask if it weren't for my book. When I managed to get to it yesterday she changed the subject almost immediately. "That time is over. What about Jim?" whom she was finally going to meet.

I turned around for a second. Yes, Kathy and Julie were right behind me, blue bathing suit next to green.

This time Sini was sitting alone in the café on the beach, reading a magazine, the newspaper in her lap, and a puzzle book for after that. I installed my kids on the sand and put lotion on them. "Of course noses need it too." I knew they wanted adventure, not this. "In fifteen days we'll go to the airport," I said, "and pick up Daddy."

What was he up to now? I had to think about that for a minute. "Maybe if it's evening," I speculated, "he might be on the living room floor trying to interest Appie in the rubber ball, but that good-for-nothing cat only runs in the direction of food." Who knows what time it was for Jim, or even what day, except of course, that "in fourteen-plus-one days Daddy will arrive." If it were Sunday morning, he'd be at the dining-room table with the slide rule and paper that he'd scribble full of numbers, "A million of them, Kathy," "more like a trillion, Julie."

I was a little older than Julie when war broke out and just about Kathy's age when I went to the Oostervelds and sat, surrounded by walls, turning eleven there and twelve and almost thirteen. If my kids looked up now they'd see an almost endless length of sky, not just the patch I could glimpse from my window. If they chose they could get up, run, "Back in a minute, Mom," or not.

What more would come up that disturbed?

"Done, all greased up." I kissed them for a second, helped to make creatures out of twigs, a feather or two, a piece of shell. Slowly I got up from the sand and joined Sini.

"New Skin Treatment," I read upside-down in her magazine. "For those who wish to appear BOLDLY attractive." She still was, I thought, more so than ever, the older she got the prettier, I told her. I knew she'd like it; she looked up. "Are you still as happy as you always claimed you were?"

"God yes, Sini," I said, wondering what she was getting at. "I couldn't ask for a sweeter husband. Each day of our marriage, almost eleven years now, he tells me 'I love you.' If only he didn't work such long hours; often the children are already asleep when he comes home. He has to, Sini, to get anywhere," I said defensively. The year before though, during the long school strike, he did manage to walk in when it was still light and without the briefcase, only to leave right after dinner for meetings on how to keep the schools open. Of course it had to be done; all kids should have a fair chance, and he was good at organizing and so articulate, controlled, and rational that even the opposition respected him. I had not liked it though, as if those nameless children of Ocean Hill-Brownsville had more of a hold on him than his own. Or than I did.

If all I could complain about was how hard he worked, it seemed, Sini said, then I was the lucky one in marriage. Thank God she was rid of David, her husband. She had had enough of tiptoeing around and trembling, anything could set him off: "How was business today?" Or: "Shall we go out tonight?"

Okay, she was getting there. He, his mother, brother, and sisters had hidden themselves during the war in an abandoned coal shed. Only David, eyes and hair just light enough to take a chance, ventured out each day, bag slung over his shoulder as if filled with tools, but containing everyone's bowel movements, which he dumped into a canal, hoping to fill the bag up again with something edible to bring back once it turned night and he dared to sneak back in.

Charles, the new boyfriend, appreciated her. "He might even move in sometime. He was hidden too and 'all that,' which is all he says about that time. This man doesn't allow the past to chase him, which suits me fine. You should see us dance, Annie ... as soon as there's something even halfway rhythmic on the radio, we get going." She demonstrated how, arms up, feet forward and sideways: a-one, a-two.

A cleaning lady, two pails in her hands as if on her way to scrub stoops, was going around the tables removing plastic tulips, dunking them in the pail with suds, swishing them around in the other, then lovingly rearranging them in the vases. Two worlds, I thought, one grafted onto the other until no one remembers where what began.

I listened to what came from the table next to ours.

They were talking of hippies sleeping against our National Monument. "The Penis," they call it. "Don't they know it's a memorial to our resistance fighters? It can't even be hosed down daily as it should be. Those youngsters won't budge." "We're too tolerant." "Same with the guest workers, our government supplementing their earnings for each new baby they seem to have fathered on a trip back to Ankara. Have we ever gone there to count?"

My mind drifted to the Oostervelds. Johan and Dientje had no children, only Sini and me, perhaps more me. Sini was already twenty when we got there.

"Annie!" She closed the magazine. "Did I tell you that the only ones who were upset when David left were the Oostervelds? You should have heard Johan when she called with the news. '*Waa*?' " making her voice sound as raucous as his must have been. " 'Goddammit, Sini, and you don't want 'm back? I don't care what you say about that man, he was a decent fellow, loved to come here. "Johan," he always said, "Tell me again what you did for those two girls. He couldn't get enough of it, Sini. *Ja*, wasn't easy for him, you had it a lot better, eh? *Waa*.' "

Her voice dropped. "Johan wants me to come to Usselo, live there again, with them. 'Of course not upstairs, Sini, I know the war's over, you don't need to rub it in, I'll fix up the shed for you, make it cozy. Just think, me and Dientje only a few steps away, keeping an eye on you, cows lowing on your other side, people like that these days, Sini, we got 'm driving over from the city just to get an earful.' "

Obviously, those people had not grown up with cattle, we laughed. We were already fed up with their sounds while still in the womb.

A memory pushes up, becomes sharper, brand new, Usselo, night time, Johan's voice at the bottom of the stairs: "Sini, come on down." Dientje protesting, and he saying: "She does need an outing, wife. We'll be back in seven minutes, twenty at the most. We're just going to put a cover on the cows, check the one's udder, see what's going on down there." I had never been allowed to come along.

Had they done anything that wasn't cow? How could I ever ask? For the book, I mean.

Sini's voice came through again. When they'd begin to fail she'd be stuck. "Who do you think will have to look after them?" She could hear Johan already: "Only Jews who weren't treated right don't need to be grateful, Sini."

"They'd be lucky," she said, "if they saw her twice a year, for their birthdays, but come late afternoon, I'm back on the train, so nothing gets to me too much. Not past, not future, Annie." She pushed the magazine into her bag, shoved the paper in as well, rubber band still around it, and went on to the puzzle book.

She didn't even know yet that I'd go there twice this time, once just for the day with Jim and again after he went back to New York, with the kids and for a week. Every night when I called Johan we talked about it. "Can't wait, Annie," as in his letters to New York after he knew I was coming. "Being with you is familiar, intimate, the past comes back up, when you were around, eh? And there was more to life than grubbing in the manure. I still know everything, don't worry, better than you and a whole lot better than Dientje, but who cares, I'll help with this book of yours, I'm good at that." (A part I had not translated for Jim—he would not want Johan to play that great a role. Just ask him the questions, you and I will take care of the rest, Jim had said.)

A few feet away, my kids were making cookies. Some got sprinkled with tobacco shreds, others with plain white sand, "a dozen square ones, please, Julie, for Mrs. Thwipplethworpe," their made-up New York name brought along to Scheveningen. "Hurry, she'll be here soon."

Good kids, very good kids, amusing themselves.

I should remind them not to hold their noses when we go

to Usselo for that week and they walk into the kitchen, and not to say "stinks," not even if they say it with a smile, Johan and Dientje might not know any English, but it was the same word in Dutch. Shouldn't forget to pack my cologne either, sprinkle some on the bed at night …

Of course they were fantastic people, Sini said, pencil still in the air, giving us life by risking theirs. Had it been up to Dientje, though, "Jews are a lot of trouble," how often had we heard that? If it hadn't been for Johan and Opoe, his mother, we wouldn't be sitting here.

We turned our faces away. We missed Opoe.

Last time I visited she was in the nursing home. "It's me, Opoe," I kept saying to the strange lady strapped into the bed, who looked but didn't recognize me, "It's Annie." I should do more, take her hand, stroke a cheek, her forehead, give a kiss. "It's me, Opoe," willing myself to recall that she came to our room when there was company in the kitchen. "I brought you something tasty too, girls," a piece of cake from under her skirt.

When a search was held and Sini and I had to crouch inside a closet all night, Opoe made sure we were still breathing and, when the enemy moved into the house too, it was Opoe who heaved herself up the stairs a few times a day just to give us a smile. "It's me, Opoe," afraid to come near her, she already looked half-gone, "It's Annie," from as far away as I could get, ready by the door, still begging for something, from me or her, but all she was interested in were the bananas I had brought. "Annie has gone to America," she insisted between mouthfuls, "And once you're there you never come back."

I didn't come back when she died. I had already been in Holland twice that year, I reasoned, for vacation, and for Father's funeral six weeks later, how could I have returned again a month after that? It would have been all right with Jim, whose mother had died the same year, 1966—a year of losses, we said that New Year's Eve and left it at that. Opoe had been a grandmother to me when I had lost mine. For Johan's sake I should have come, to have stood next to Sini. And for myself, so I wouldn't be sitting on this beach feeling shame.

Not that it was important, Sini said, but had there been no war and no Johan, which was one and the same, had she not been so scared afterward and tired of figuring out what to do with her freedom, she would never have married David. It had to be a Jew, that was clear, so close after the war. "What if during a fight he hurled 'Dirty Jew' at me, or even worse, had he known about me 'then,' would he have turned me in?" David was so capable, she thought, considering what he had done, taken care of his whole family. Even his looks reminded her of Johan, peasant-y sort of.

What happens, Sini wondered, when one of them dies? "Am I supposed to take in the one that's left behind?" If it is Dientje, she'd better learn what a bathtub is for. The only time they ever came to visit, they stayed for a week, not that they wanted to, but everyone in Usselo would've ridiculed them had they returned any sooner. "Sini sent you back already, after all you've done?" Every day of that week Sini had to explain how the bathtub worked, "put in plug, turn on faucet, and climb in." Dientje refused to even look: "I wait till I get back home, Sini, wash my hands under the pump."

And if it were Johan who lived longer, each day would be rehashed, all one thousand of them, when he was the rescuer and she had no voice. Determined, Sini kept turning the pages of her puzzle book until she found one she liked, the kind without any interruption of black squares. "It's easy for you, Annie, all you have to do is come to the funeral."

The sun was relentless. No cloud, none was approaching, none had been announced, not even low pressure from somewhere over Ireland or Scotland, where normally the bad weather came from.

I thought about all those times in New York when I had sat with a pad, writing down questions for Johan. That very first evening, cold, I remember, when Sini and I barged in, just like that, we were afraid. Had you wanted us?

If the weather would be even halfway nice the week of the visit, we'd sit on the bench, Johan and I, he bent all the way forward until his back was horizontal with arms on his knees and a piece of wet cigar between thick fingers. There was a bench we often sat at between the outhouse and the walnut tree, in the grassy spot he called "pavilion" from where you could also see the linden tree, tall, growing beyond the window that used to be mine, the left one.

I wouldn't have to ask Johan when the leaves fall, nor what they looked like, egg-shaped, spikes all around the edge. I once counted 118 on a leaf closest to my chair. It was full of holes, as if hit by needles.

"Remember that storm, Johan, when you weren't sure that tree would make it? The nest, though, I could never spot no matter how I craned my neck. It was a nest of wood pigeons that returned each May, to lay eggs, two, you said, light-gray. Where exactly? I want to be sure I get it right for my book." The feeling of closeness was coming back, of being the kid who with him always felt safe. I could already see myself sitting there with him, my children rushing by, carrying bowls of milk after kittens that were mousers and always on the run. They'd shriek if wasps rose from the piles of rotten apples that were everywhere. "Help, Mom!" And Johan

would laugh: "Ah, city kids, what do they know about life?"
Sometimes Dientje would stop reading her book, *Love in the
Emergency Room* or some such, and come to the window
of the good room, not to open it—"Drafts make you sick"—
but to peer out. "Come in, Johan, pneumonia will hit, already you don't look right," her finger climbing out of the
nostril—I should warn Jim about that habit of hers: "As soon
as she sits, her finger goes right up her nose, you'll see"—or
she'd be shouting something else through the glass, "Ever
clean your house, Annie, or don't they do that in America?"
Or a neighbor would stop by, talk a little about grass, the
price of milk, no good either. And we'd go on again, Johan
and I, as soon as we could.

A whole week there, though ... pump, outhouse, my hair
standing up in oily peaks. Last time, when I spent only three
full days and asked Johan if I could go to the neighbors' across
the road and use their shower, he became angry. "During the
war this house was good enough for you."

What am I going to do there for seven evenings? Stare at
the flypaper hanging from the ceiling, count how many dead,
guess how quickly those still wriggling will give up, watch Dientje kill live ones with those huge hands of hers? Once war
had been discussed, there'd be nothing left to say. I'd look at
my watch, stealthily, "Going to bed soon," I think. Johan's
"Not yet, Annie, stay up a little longer," his eyes lonelier, his
voice more urgent as the week creeps on. Perhaps the phone
would ring, and he'd order me to answer it. Why, I'd ask,
it's not for me, but I'd get up anyway, say "Hello," and hand
him the receiver. "That was Annie," he'd beam, "Our little
person-in-hiding I told you about, Can't forget me, you're
right, came all the way from America, *Nef Yo'k, ja*, just to
hear what I've got to say."

I would never stay in Usselo for a week if it weren't for my book: I wouldn't even want to hear about war if it weren't for that. After which, pad filled with answers, I'd be off, and he'd say, on my way out, "It'll be years before we can see you again, three, you think? Who knows if we'll be around by then?"

I touched my face. Sand. Sweat. And who knew what else. Guilt. Or even anger, hidden still.

If I ever were to do this—*write*—and leave his name just as it was, Johan Oosterveld, would he like that?

THE CONDUCTOR RAISED his stop-go signal, he whistled, and the train began to pull out of Rachel's city, Amersfoort, in the middle of Holland. Another wave, one more "thank you, Tante," from my girls, but she had already hurried off the platform. Rachel did not like good-byes.

We walked along the corridor until we found seats. On the wall of the compartment were a mirror and two prints, one of saints, the other one of a bar where a blond woman sat on a stool, looking sad.

Kathy opened her book about life on the prairie, back home, tightly holding on to King John, her stuffed dog, still worried probably that Julie, even now, ready to doze off, would attack him again; already she had yanked out his tongue. He looked strange with his new one, much too small, more befitting Julie's frog, to whom it had belonged until she felt sorry for what she had done and wanted to make up.

I put our bags on the rack and settled in. From the waste-basket underneath the window newspapers stuck out filled with yesterday's moon landing, the first ever. July 20, 1969. "Congratulations, America, we knew you could do it." Others questioned, "If God had wanted us there, wouldn't the Bible have said so?"

Again I wondered whether Jim had watched the astronauts on television, and where. In his office? He would have loved seeing on screen what up until then had only seemed an imaginary place, like the country, name unpronounceable, that he and his friend from the office imagined whenever he brought him home. Long after I had gone to bed— "Goodnight, Jim." "Goodnight, Pat." Did they even notice I had said something?—I could hear them leap around their other world, whose supreme achievement would be the rational ordering of everything imaginable, where four weeks made a month, of which thirteen made a year, that extra one called Month of Storms.

The train picked up speed and the Amersfoort station receded. We were passing an industrial complex now, still in scaffolds, where elm, oak, and ash trees used to grow. I was glad Jim would get to see Holland before it was all cemented together. There, finally, countryside, meadows, a farmhouse surrounded by fruit trees and dahlias already unfolding due to the heat. And, look, at the edge of the roadbed, right under my eyes, broom bushes, every flower shaped like a butterfly, and rowan trees, berries tinted with orange, it wasn't even August yet. Beyond where we just passed, stretches of yellow. "Why don't you look outside, Kathy and Julie, it's so beautiful." They nodded, never raising their heads. I should be thankful they weren't giving me a hard time; it wasn't easy for them to be away from their friends and only have each other for company. That's how it had been for Sini and me, creating a bond that was still with us. Did it have to be something like war to create that kind of closeness? Or would any trauma do? Hopefully Kathy and Julie would not have to experience that either. What actually did it take? In Jim's family, his father's leaving and his mother's illness surely didn't do it. When Jim and Phil and their sister got together at their father's home outside Washington, they acted as if they had just met at a railroad station with time to spare for a discussion, a debate about government procedures, say, or the politics of erecting a new building, or the ethics of something else.

Intently I looked out, as I knew Sini would, for a blue heron, head wedged between his shoulders, standing at the side of a ditch, stock-still, until a bite to eat appeared and it would pounce. She drew them, lone creatures in a silent landscape watched over by a tree, a pollard willow like the one that just went by, or something more spindly on which she would draw a human face expressing envy that those birds knew exactly what they wanted. And could wait for it too.

My thoughts went to Rachel, who by now must be back home, in her living room filled with empty chairs, embroidering or knitting and checking the clocks a hundred times a day—how many more hours till nighttime?—as if there were still war with only the New Testament for company, provided by the minister who not only saved her life but gave her his religion too; as she must have counted the hours afterwards in the TB sanatorium she ended up in. When finally she was healthy again, she married and moved to Amersfoort, where she came to dread nighttime as well. Her husband in his sleep screamed for his mother who, way back "then," having received an offer for just one hiding place and without money that might have provided more, decided that he, Niek, Rachel's husband, should be given the chance to survive. "Your father and I will go off to camp, you're still young." The doctor was going to try a small dose of LSD on Niek, Rachel said, and there'd be a chance he'd open up.

If it weren't for those thousand days and nights of having been tucked away from the reach of trains—with good results, as they said of us afterward—how different would we have turned out?

Like father's brothers and sisters. Had there been ten? Most of the men cattle dealers begrudging the other's bargain cow. I began to check off those relatives I knew or had heard about. Uncle Mozes, in pants big as sails, who used to select his own potato at the greengrocer's, his doctor had told him only one a day, but not what size; the same uncle who said babies grew in his turnip patch. And there was the uncle who liked to be tickled up and down his arm, but really wanted to be a swimmer. Marjan who sold kosher merchandise—only buy what's packaged, shoppers whispered; she has a drippy nose for which she ate garlic. Then the aunt who burned her sauerkraut after her unmarried daughter announced that she was pregnant. And there was Aunt Rose—*sshht*, the prostitute—thank God, all the way over in Amsterdam, and Uncle Jacob whose wife had rheumatism in her hands, which angered him so that he never talked to her, but who yelled "Stop hurting her, she's already in pain" when the enemy dragged her onto the train, an extra one that day, at night, the dejudification process needed speeding up.

Had they all been taken to the same camp? When they could no longer fight over money, who should've had more, who deserved less or none at all, when all of that fell away, were they able to comfort one another?

Outside, a windmill without vanes passed by the train, amidst grass dull green and dusty. If you moved your eyes up you could see a band of yellow forming around the sun. It looked almost like the onset of rain. It lifted some and a light began to show, hushed, mystic almost, gilding whatever lay below. "Kathy, Julie, pick up your heads." They did, for a second. Didn't they want to take a better look? A little longer one? Of course, they knew about the light in Holland from museums their father had taken them to. Still, now they could see it for real ...

"Could you live here again?" Sini asked last week, Rachel just this morning. "I don't know," I answered. Anyway, how could I? "I'm married to an American and I've lived there for such a long time ..." Although lately, I wasn't sure why, I had been telling Jim I'd like to live on a farm. "It doesn't have to be big, the Oostervelds' size would be fine." But not in the country, I wanted a farm right in Manhattan, at our very same address.

I suddenly recalled the dream I had the night before, while still in Amersfoort, staying at Rachel's. Had it been after hearing Niek scream? I was on my way to Usselo. I could see the road, the bend, I could spot Johan's and Dientje's house, but I wasn't getting any closer, to Winterswijk, yes, where I had not meant to go at all ... I had no coat, no shoes, no place to stay. "Let's go to a hotel," I said to Rachel and Sini, "I'll pay." They weren't even with me. Neither had I been traveling with my kids. I looked at them. They were right here, practically sitting on top of me. I put my cheek on their heads. They knew I loved them, didn't they?

The train clattered on, past banks of heather, all purple, interspersed with yellow sandhills and masses of pine trees. Somewhere inside that darkness used to be an underground village built by Jews, eighty of them, who were discovered near the end by soldiers who had only been hunting for deer.

And on, past yellow sand roads where, during the last winter of war when people in the big cities had been dying of hunger, those still strong enough had walked in shoes without soles, pushing a doll's carriage here, a stroller there, with sheets in them, a wedding dress, begging farmers to "please" give them something in exchange, an ounce of sugar, a handful of wheat, a potato or two, but quick, they needed to return before it was too late. That same winter my father, at night, sneaked around alleyways on the lookout for a stray dog to catch and bring back to his hiding address, where he would butcher it. His rescuers also had bread, paid for with his money. He did not ask to share, as he always made sure to lose the nightly game of cards they played with him, and they could say, "No luck again, de Leeuw. Maybe tomorrow." What was I doing here for seven weeks that couldn't have been done in four, or less? Or from comfortably far away, in my own living room, where I could have made up what was missing. All this digging like a mole, deeper and farther …

In my mind's eye I searched for Jim's face, aglow against the stretch of candlelight the evening we said yes, I should go, not only to see my family but to steep myself in that other time. It wouldn't be easy, we said. Reliving never is. It would be worth it, we said again.

. I crossed my arms and pressed them to my chest as if to keep myself together. Never before had I felt this raw, not even in 1966, when I sped over to Father's funeral; not when Mother died while I was already in hiding. A few sobs, that was all. Better, I said to Sini, repeating it to Johan and Dientje and Opoe, and to myself. All better, until I too believed it.

Two people walked by our compartment, looked in, and continued on their way. I heard a train going in the opposite direction. Ours click-clacked on, farther east, toward Winterswijk, where my war broke out and would again, only I didn't know it yet. That's where I was when the phone call came. *Sshht.* At my stepmother's house, it was still night; I was in bed asleep, as were my children. *Sshht,* the phone call that keeps piercing my ears no matter how densely I pad them.

I got up, stood by the window, and looked. For what, this time? We might already have passed the town where I taught for two years, fresh out of college, forty-six first graders, from very smart to Mientje, who, at the end of the school year still thought that one and one made something other than two. My goodness, she must be in her twenties by now. Was she still watering begonias all day as she had in my classroom? Flooding saucers. She had not been retarded in every way, though. At an age when I barely knew I had a vagina, let alone what it was for, she already had an infection "down there," due to newspapers and other wads she had pushed in. Maybe she thought of it as a saucer that needed to be mopped.

I wondered about another child—Henkie. Had he learned to wash, to blow his nose in something other than his hand, not to hiss into every neck he could reach? Had he learned that standing on a chair, arms out and roaring "*Grrrr*, Miss de Leeuw," wasn't appropriate? He gave me a present when I left, a yellowed card of a Boeing bomber, aloft. I brought it with me when I came to America, in the trunk labeled DESTINATION HOBOKEN USA. I was sad when I quit, but my hands were covered with eczema; I stood by the blackboard and scratched. The job was too much for me, the doctor said.

I remembered Jim's hives when he went to work for the retail firm, a huge one I was so happy with, that gave him raises when they said they would, as though they wrote the promise down on a calendar page. He had hives everywhere, lips, ears, around his eyes; there were even hives on his genitals. An allergy, apparently. To what we didn't find out. And kidney stones, he had those too in that first month and I was so afraid they'd tell him to get out. Or that he wanted to, and look for something else again, where he was needed more. Another business doomed to fail, I'd think. So far not a peep out of him about changing, four years with the same company, a record ...

The train chugged past more parched grass and piles of hay that, instead of being saved for winter, were already being used. An old farmer feeding a pig slop from a pail. Through the window across the corridor an intersection of two streets. A bicyclist, crocheted cover across the seat to prevent her clothes from turning shiny as she shifted from side to side. And tiny plots made available by the government for people who had no gardens of their own. Someone stopped hoeing a row of beans and raised his rake. I waved back.

In seven days, Jim was going to come and we'd start all over again, visiting and crisscrossing through Holland. He'd love it. About the year he lived in France, when someone asked him, "What was it like, your Fulbright?," the first thing he'd say was, "I rode the trains a lot." As soon as he had a break from school, Sciences Po, and some francs in his pocket, he'd board a train and take it as far as his money went.

His mother was still in the hospital then, wasn't she? Her fourth year? Or the beginning of the fifth? Sometimes, on a Saturday afternoon after his work, he'd walk with the kids to a store near us filled with trains, green and blue and yellow, and the very dark, almost black Pennsylvania Railroad models. They'd watch these miniatures loop in and out of tunnels, Jim with his nose pushed against the window, face cocked to one side as though he expected a whistle or honking, an echo from long ago, from Christmas maybe, when his family still lived in a big house in Philadelphia and a train was set up around their tree. Or less far back in time, after his parents' breakup, when his father would visit him, his brother, and Lucy, his sister, in the tiny house along the Delaware Canal they had moved to with their mother, at Lock No. 12, the Delaware River right across the towpath, where he played war games with the local boys, Nazis versus Allies. He took us there once, did my kids remember? "Kathy? Julie?" To whom was I addressing myself anyway, one of them frowning over a page, the other sound asleep, or pretending to be. A beautiful September Sunday it had been, with winter still far away, and no autumn mists yet that would shroud the poplars and sycamores bordering the river, where, he said, at times the fog would sit and just touch the water, which would be all black, and you had to be careful not to stumble in.

That same river his mother sketched day and night, trying to get it right, and a neighbor lady would stop and compare the sketches to her brownies. It's not only your baking, Idy, that needs practice, she'd say to Jim's mother.

When we had visited, Jim had showed us where the rowboat was kept, pointing at a bit of grass alongside the house. A leaky boat he'd get into after school, a scrawny boy, his belt pulled so tightly around his pants you wondered how he could breathe. Perfect for sitting in, he said, pretending he was on a voyage, or that it was Friday and Bob, his father, was on the train. At a sharp curve in the roadbed it would shrill, that's when he'd come and Jim would run to the front of the house so he'd be the first one to see him. Until the visits stopped. Phil, his brother, went to live with his father and his father's new wife, his sister Lucy left with a boyfriend, and Jim, who was thirteen then, moved with his mother to a village closer to the sound of trains, three a day rumbled by their window. He could hear them, perched on the sill. And freight trains whenever they had a load of coal.

I checked my face in the mirror opposite my seat. I had become too thin, my sisters said. Perhaps a little hollow under the eyes? And sad, they told me. Quickly I slouched down. I worked too hard, that must be it, always trying to find something to translate, either from the Dutch or into it, to bring in extra money. I even baked our own bread, and now also trying to write ... no, nothing was wrong, I had a good life. It hadn't always been easy, that I had to admit. All those jobs Jim had slaved away at for little pay, Kathy born, Julie born, his student loan, his mother who needed money, my family too far away to visit ... where had he found those jobs, from the first one at the department store in Detroit that refused to pull through, to the company that made hats—with or without dents—that no one wore, where he'd work even on a Saturday night. No more, I said after another phone call, announcing: "Can't leave yet. But soon." Which wasn't soon at all, and I had to cancel the sitter for the fourth Saturday in a row.

"That's it, Jim, you have a family. You're not like your boss, who's in no hurry to get back to an empty room. You have a home." He had just gotten there, he was sitting on the edge of the bed, taking off his shoes. "We were exploring ways of reducing inventory, Ann, and different strategies to stop sales from slipping even more. If all goes well we may finally see some cautious growth."

"Maybe," I said, "Or maybe not. You're always telling me there's hope for the next quarter or for the Christmas season or Mother's Day or Father's Day. I can't stand it anymore. This place probably won't be any different from the others, another Chapter Eleven coming up. Can't you stop trying to rescue businesses that are already dead by the time you get there? I want you to look for another job. As long as you work this hard, at least let it be for a firm that doesn't milk you dry."

His shoes were going back on. What had I unleashed? One shoe, the other one. He got off the bed and put his jacket on too. "Are you leaving?" I asked, my voice as soft now as his had been. "Where are you going? At this hour?" For a walk. "Is what I said so awful that you need to get away? Are you angry?" Although anger was not what his face showed, he looked beaten. "No, how could I be angry? I don't blame you, Ann. It's time I became an adult."

I sat up until I heard the key in the door. We hugged. I cried. "I'll look for a different job," he said. "It may take a while, though; you need to be patient." After not long at all, within a few months, he had already found something at the firm with the promise of raises kept, which a year ago went into a new kind of business, insurance, Jim being one of only four people in it. At the helm of a ship, we said, excited. "Anything that company touches grows, they can't help it, Jim," and with his credentials—Yale, Harvard Business School, the political studies year in France, he couldn't miss ...

I beamed at the scenery outside the train again, stalks and sprigs of this and that, a field of cabbage, a length of yellow, a form of ranunculus? And dots of pink along a stretch of water too wide for a ditch. Would there be a letter from Jim waiting in Winterswijk, as there had been at Rachel's? He was doing well, he wrote, he missed us, saw friends, enjoyed the cat, practiced his Dutch, and still had a lot to do before he could get on the plane, a project had to be finished, something about convertible debentures, whatever they were, important no doubt.

How is it possible, I sometimes thought, that I, brought up with cows, am married to someone to whom they meant nothing more than a tasty bite, while I still saw the hide that had wrapped it, hooves, a tail trying to sweep off flies? And the udder that solemnly swung back and forth.

The man who had passed our compartment before was back, followed by the same woman—his wife? They even looked alike. That's what happened, Sini said, the way a dog often resembles his owner. You wonder, is that why they picked each other? Did they still make love? Another question you could never ask anyone. Dientje once volunteered: "Johan never bothered me much. He was very nice that way." Of course when Sini and I were there, nothing could be done, with me in the same bed and Sini on the floor next to it. Had it ever been unduly noisy? Any breathing that implied coupling in spite of the odds?

For a while I thought of nothing, not of bed, not of a mattress on the floor next to it, who was in it or on it, or who got up to urinate or whatever.

Julie was holding King John now, and Kathy was stroking the tongueless frog. The train puffed past more sleepy villages. In some I had worked, a day or two, a week, until the teacher I took over from got better and I'd have to tell them at home, No, tomorrow I wasn't working, and I might not be for a while, either. What if I looked for something different; I had trouble keeping order in a classroom. Sometimes the principal would come in, "Please, Miss de Leeuw, keep the noise down, it's disturbing others." What if, for a while at least, I'd do some waitressing? "Our kind of people," my stepmother said—ignoring that my father always came home with manure on his shoes and pants—"are above working in a restaurant," and I knew I had to give up that idea, her hands were already clutching her throat, a sure sign that an attack was on the way, asthma, an illness that had started during the war, which she survived hidden in a room dug beneath stabled cows, where, at times, she'd get splattered by dung.

As we approached a wheat field, a flock of crows rose up, wings flapping wildly, and I saw cows waiting by a gate to be milked. I could hear them too, or was it because I knew they'd be lowing? If any of them had been Father's, no matter for how short a time, he would've known all about them, prone to what disease, jittery or not, a lot more than he ever knew or cared to know about his children, Rachel and Sini said when the three of us had spent a day together in Scheveningen.

I floated back, hearing their voices again. In a meadow, Father never seemed ready to take off; there he could be standing as if he had all the time in the world, they said, "He could've used some of that at home, instead of jumping up and barking, 'Good-bye, girls. Take care of everything, the house. And of your mother too.'" With her in the hospital he was exempt, the soldiers wouldn't have come for him. "It was smart not to trust," I had to defend him. They knew as well as I did that men were lifted out of their beds and dragged off way before women. "And he didn't go into hiding until he had found addresses for us too." Triumphantly, I looked at them. "He took off before," they answered, relentless, "For Switzerland, don't you remember?" All but tripping over their words now. "One minute he announced: 'Someday I might. I'm thinking about it.' Next minute he was out the door. Slam, gone." Sini jumped up, acting it out. He wasn't much of a Father, they concluded. "Can you imagine, he once took me with him to the slaughterhouse?" Sini said, still shocked. "I was only six. Until this day I can't stand the sight of meat, and if I was the one sent out to buy it, I had it wrapped in so many layers of newspaper that I couldn't feel what was inside." "Had he been successful," I said, still digesting Switzerland, "he would have sent for us." They did not agree with me there either, they were rolling their eyes. "It's true," I protested, "Someone was going to come, and take us to a barge that would whisk us along the Rhine, through Germany, over to Basel, up to his alp."

"Where cows wore bells," they scoffed. "The only kind of music he liked. Have no illusions, we'd never have seen him again." "How do we know he wouldn't have done anything to get us there," I said. "Had he not been stopped at the border?" They wouldn't let up. "You remember his face when he walked back in, don't you? It wasn't one of happiness that he was back with us." "Everything was abnormal," I said, half in tears. "It was war." "Which gave him what he wanted," they answered, "A way out of a terrible marriage. To think that he waited two years for her …" They couldn't stop laughing. "Met her in some village at 18." "Must've liked what he saw." "And told her, 'When you turn twenty, I'll be back and marry you.' " Would have been better had he not kept his word," Rachel thought. He, adventurous, Mother, whiny, or queasy, eyes on her embroidery, cross-stiches learned from nuns." Nuns? I had no idea she was educated by nuns. What else would they come up with? Fights, they said, didn't I ever hear them? "Yes," that I had to admit, "but having to do with the war. 'Let's go to America, Sophie.' That was sensible." All right, maybe he had had no trouble leaving mother, but didn't we count? Meaning "didn't I?" which I was afraid to ask. "Not even you," they guessed, his favorite, cute—they always say that about the youngest—whom he'd join in the playpen, slapping the palm of his hand onto mine, mine onto his, he even hummed, granted the only thing he knew, still it was a song, *O du lieber Augustin*, Grab what you can from life, it won't last." Jopie, they said, our brother, "When he died, barely out of high school, poor thing, that hurt." "The Lord takes the good ones first," Rachel said.

There was more I learned that day that Rachel came to Scheveningen, or learned again, I don't know. Across the water, much farther away than we could see—we had walked to the beach by then—was England. Jews tried to scramble there after the invasion, my sisters said, in boats that left from Scheveningen, close to the beach café Sini liked. Father wouldn't have taken us there either, they said, pointing toward the horizon where I, doggedly, kept conjuring up the playpen, only my father and me in it, I pulling his moustache, he beaming and humming the song he knew.

Other memories are breaking in, more of what I heard that day. "Imagine," Sini and Rachel laughed, "When you were born we had to bring roses to the hospital, show Mother we too were delighted with the 'aftercomer.' Remember, Sini, we once dropped her?" Rachel still seemed to think it was funny. "People in the street kept screaming, 'Watch it, you're running too fast.'" "At the marketplace," Sini said, "which now, Annie, you'll see, swarms with Germans who come across the border, with their cars empty, prices are lower here, and lower yet for Winterswijkers who stand around grinning." "Behind the church where cows got sold, that's where the carriage toppled. Ooh, we yelled, here comes his little calf, up for sale. It could have injured your brain, they said, we were lucky there."

"When it was all over, he was happy to see us, Sini. That

you remember, don't you? He stood in the Oosterveld kitchen and cried." We barely recognized the hollowed-out man who claimed us. Johan had become my father, not this mustachioed apparition who kept wiping his eyes but wouldn't sit down. "Let's go home, come, it's time for you to leave."

"Just a minute," Johan protested, "I can't let you take them yet. The roads are still dangerous, there are mines out there, they say, and unexploded bombs. I need to travel to Winterswijk first, make sure it's safe. I got 'm through the war, Ies," he told Father. "I'm not letting anything happen to 'm now."

I didn't remind Sini and Rachel that a few months after the war—or had it only been weeks?—Father remarried. I was still 13, and Sini had left Winterswijk. Father told Rachel—he knew she'd be critical—to move out. "Here's your new mother, Annie. Be nice to Magda, she hasn't had it easy. Just do as she says."

I jolted forward, aware of the noise of a train again and that my children wanted something. A busy sky, I agreed, looking out and up too. Patches of light and dark, and darker yet that changed as they traveled, becoming wisps, puffs, until it was one blanket of gray that unraveled again.

"You're right, a busy sky. Shall I tell you something, Kathy, Julie, about the sky in Holland? Ten years after the war had ended, it rained daffodils over The Hague, dropped by British planes, yes, a celebration. People stood on rooftops and sidewalks trying to guess where exactly the flowers would fall, so they could catch one, like holding the sun in your very own arms, yes.

"I know, Julie, it's been a long sit, but in two stops we get off. Oma will be waiting at the station with the car. You're right, not Opa. We have to be especially nice to Oma now that she lives alone." They nodded. Where were his ponies,

named after them? Ketty and Shullie, he used to say. "Sold,"
I said. "And no more cows either." Did we look all right? Not
too wrinkled? That could easily happen on a trip, and she so
particular. I checked the children, then myself, taking extra
care now, flicking at specks that may not have been there at
all. What were they going to say to her? A stream of words
came out, all Dutch: hello, carrot, cookie, pig, horse, I'm hun-
gry, I've had enough, thank you, good morning, and may we
have a peeled grapefruit. She'd love it, even if crumbs fell onto
the velvet of her chairs, she'd call them cuties and tell me they
didn't resemble me at all. And Jim she admired. At the wedding she'd stared at him, wordless. Classy, her eyes said.

The smell of manure drifted in through the open window.
My kids began to count horses, "Only brown ones, Julie, or
there'll be too many."

I kept looking at my watch. It struck me how much longer it would stay light here, until way after nine, when hours
of darkness had already stretched over New York. "Shall we
send Daddy a have-a-good-trip letter tonight?" I asked. "He'll
get it just before he leaves. And "Tell him," my kids rattled,
"That Tante Rachel is knitting us sweaters with bears, and
we'll tell him about the bees in her yard, we trapped one in
a cup, that he should give Appie a kiss, scratch him under
the chin, between the ears and on his belly too." Yes, all of
that could go into the letter. Welcome to the country of my
youth, I'd add.

The edge of my town was about to appear, a rim of woods,
the Jewish cemetery behind it. My brother Jopie was buried
there; my mother; Father; where spaces meant for other Winterswijk Jews would never be filled. *Yisgadal v'yiskadash*,
extolled and hallowed, *sh'ma rabbo*, be the name of God.

If you followed the path that led from the cemetery and
went around the bend where the road became paved, you

saw poplars swaying high above ditches and meadows that used to be Father's, where on a summer's day when no rain had fallen I pumped water into a stone trough for his cows. And from where, whip in hand, whenever father's laborer was working for someone else or had been drunk, I prodded a cow onto the road and walked it over to the farmer Father had sold it to. It was the same road on which the two houses sat, both white and across from each other. One I came back to after the war, and the smaller one built right after I went to America. They weren't counting on me to live at home again. "The white bungalow," Magda called it when giving her address in city shops. "That's all the post office needs, no one else in Winterswijk has a home like that."

You could find rye fields along that road too, in which cornflowers grew and poppies and yellow ox-eyed daisies. "With luck we'll find enough to make a wreath and you could be haloed princesses as we gallop into town." Yes, I'd give them a little money for a trinket they had to have, but only if they went into a store by themselves and asked for it in Dutch, which, of course again, I'd write down for them on a piece of paper, one for each if necessary. "We could just show it, Mom." I laughed. We'd have fun. I'd take them to the swimming pool where, hopefully, local kids more accustomed to blond than to dark wouldn't pelt them with sand again, as they had on the previous trip. We'd visit Oma's friends, including Mrs. Menko. "Absolutely," they shouted, having been in camp, she understood that pastries should be offered the minute they walked in. And maybe Oma's blackcurrants were ripe, and a gooseberry or two ...

AT THE END of the road, across the railroad tracks, the town began. First came the slaughterhouse, a busy place, especially early on Tuesdays, unlike the yard of the tombstone cutter, which bustled each night when, behind slabs of stone waiting to be shaped, kissing was practiced—French, the rumor went, a wet business and not for everyone.

If you crossed the street again, you'd be at the Catholic cemetery with the warning on the gate, HODIE MIHI, CRAS TIHI. (Today me, tomorrow you.) A little beyond, I used to play with Margo, Elly, Carla, my cousin Hannie, hopscotch and marbles, a star on each of our chests, yellow but not pretty, and with whom I spied, between the legs of a lady lounging on a chair outside her door, no underpants. We'd bend down pretending we were looking for something else, wondering would that be our future too, something hairy where you wouldn't expect it. That same lady joined my playmates on the one-way train, waving See you, to almost no one there. It was early when it left, on schedule, always, at the hour trucks stopped at the slaughterhouse with a delivery of calves.

On the same cobblestone street, close to the cemetery reminding us tomorrow might be us, was the dance school I went to after the war. "It'll do you good," my father said. "Maybe you'll lose some of your seriousness." Those tangos ... such beautiful music, it almost brought tears to my eyes as I waited for the instructor who, in his prewar black suit that had survived hiding along with him, pushed the girls across the floor himself. "Come," as he positioned me away from the wall, "isn't it great we can do this again?"

On, deeper into town, over to the area where birds in the window of "Song Seeds" chirped as live advertisements, a few doors from the bakery where Father's car once smashed the door and wall, half a block away from where I started off in life, at Stationstraat number 3, very close to the railroad terminal and the park alongside it, full of beeches, swastikas carved into the trunks of some. Those I avoid in the fall when picking up nuts from the ground, they could make you sick, like certain berries I threatened to eat when I didn't get my way.

At the front of the station was the candy machine, bright red, which dispensed sugar balls that constantly changed color, every few seconds you'd have to spit it into your hand and check, what shade now? The very last time I saw my mother, she gave me a coin for it. I took it with me into hiding, together with the purse she put it in.

I should have brought it on this trip, something of hers to hold as I used to grip her hand on Saturdays when we went to the synagogue. Father's orders, "Get up and go, Sophie. It matters." Why, he doesn't explain; he's already halfway there.

Mother doesn't walk fast; that's good, it makes the out-ing last for a while, around the park, the station, then a left at the street. She carries her umbrella on the side I'm not on, blue, same dark shade as her raincoat, which she wears even when the sun is out and not a cloud can be found. We meet my grandmother inside the *shul* where I climb the stairs behind my friend Alie, a white bow already crumpled at her neck. Carla is there too, she knows how to kiss a boy. You need your tongue, she says, licklicklick, which I might be doing to a chocolate round—if cousin Hannie re-members to bring me one, from her own supply. After syna-gogue, hands dangling empty, I go down the stairs again, back onto the same street, deathly silent now. That's when you hear it, *tftftf*, a train arriving from Germany, maybe Jews on it with bundles. They want to get off, live here until safer days reach them, police may not let them, might be waiting on the platform to prod them back on for the trip in reverse.

I see my house, as clearly as if I'm already in front of it, Number 3, at the end of a row of houses all shaped alike, only on my doorpost a *mezuzah* I'm supposed to look at as I walk in. *Sshht*, it's dark, Mother might be resting, on the sofa underneath the red cover strewn with petals, black, as in just before they drop.

Or, something else I remember, I am smaller again—five?—the drapes are only half drawn, letting in some light, enough for Mother's needle and cloth, and to see the milk-man approach when I, pan in hand, am allowed to show him how much milk we need that day, but walking carefully, once away from the house things can happen to you, Mother says. "There are automobiles, especially your father's, there are bicycles and horse-drawn carts that can do you in."

If Mother's headaches, there's more than one, she says,

have not yet arrived, she lets me pull at the string of the music box that's resting on the mahogany chest, a melody tingletangles forth and the ship inside the glass dome begins to sway. The harder I pull—"Gently!"—the wilder the waves become, like the milk I slosh around the pan. From the back room I can see our yard, a frame in the middle over which the rugs get flung for the weekly beating done with a length of rattan wielded by our cleaning lady, who has an extra toe on one foot that her boyfriend, *sshht*, knows nothing about.

There is also a pear tree where Rachel and Sini, when it's shabbos and you shall not pick, stand on a chair, mouths open, teeth groping toward something ripe, leaving the cores to shrivel on the twigs, from one Saturday to the next. Sometimes they lift me so I too can eat a pear. I do, after checking the neighbor's beehives aren't open, ready to punish.

Bordering our yard on the other side is a corner of old van der Wal's, the neighbor who likes to expose himself between the peach tree and the rosebush, show his *schlemazzel*, Sini says, giving it a Hebrew sound that Father makes on Friday evenings when we sit around the table laid with a white cloth, damask, a pattern of roses woven through it.

He prays quickly, swallowing half of the bobbledebobbles to speed it up even more. My brother, Jopie, listens carefully, so that later, when he's grown up and has to lead, he'll know how.

Each time Sini hears a syllable that reminds her of old van der Wal, she giggles and Father taps her on the head with the blunt side of his knife; Rachel tries to catch him in a mistake and sneak an extra sip from the one glass of wine that's passed around, which makes Mother say, "If this swilling won't stop, you'll turn into a sot."

I'm allowed to say something at the seder, a solo, in Hebrew, about a different night, *halailoh hazeh*. Father nods, I said it right; Mother looks happy, as when she hears Jopie practice the violin and she plays the piano, her hands gliding across the keys, lightly, nothing more than brushing air. A cradle song? Is that what I'm hearing now? Yes, her body is rocking from side to side. I begin to dance, my legs are moving, a few steps here, there, a stick in my hand is doing the same, pompom. I stay on the rug, close to her, I want to see it all, the fast notes that have flags, the slow ones that look back at you wide-eyed, her hands, her face, half of which is down toward the sounds she's making, the other half she keeps up, receiving them. I want to see everything before she slips back to the sofa and huddles underneath the cover that is partially red. Where she stays after Jopie dies, a ruptured appendix, our drapes closed without a break, preventing even as much as a glint of light. It's gloomy everywhere, no more music, even after Jopie is buried and weeks go by, the piano stays mum. All you can hear is soldiers strutting through the Stationstraat, where doors open to let out greetings in the language of the conquerors. Who knows what Jopie has been spared, Uncle Mozes whispered, mouthful of mourning, *Yisgadal v'yiskadash*.

* * *

The train wheels click. I look out but no station, no park, and no view yet of the house, frozen behind drapes, where I spent the first nine years of my life. My mind begins to race as my body did that night in 1940, when a firebomb aimed at the station fell on nearby sheds. Someone—who?—woke me up and walked me down the stairs into the street. I have a blanket around me, I've been sick, I shouldn't even be out, night air is the worst, Mother says. I hear a swishing noise, a thud, then silence. The air-raid alarm goes off. "Why only now?" people scream, "What if a gas main broke?" The fire spreads. Away to where we can't feel the flames, before they stretch out and claw us. Quick, to where the sky is less red. I'm pulled along by Sini and Rachel, who also tugs at Mother's hand to make sure she doesn't turn around and go back home. It is still so light, I see it all, there, old van der Wal in a nightshirt, his wife wearing one just like his, only longer, her buttocks don't show.

And I see the silhouette of a man running faster than anyone. I squeeze my eyes shut, I pull the folds of drapes across, I cover them with Mother's petals, but extra lids don't help, not anymore. Whatever illusion I had still clung to is gone. There he is, my father, way ahead, dark pants held up by suspenders and ending in slippers, edges fuzzy. Clapclap, gigglegiggle, big hand onto tiny palm, tiny palm patting big one. He never looks back to see whether we, whether I, will be safe. The best child in the world ...

I no longer know where I am, with whom, or why I got myself into this. My kids' voices are coming through, "Winterswijk, Mom, the conductor just announced. We need to get off." The train crunches to a halt. In the town where it all began. Birth. Death. War. And being walked out on.

THE UNUSUAL WEATHER HELD. There was no longer even a suggestion of drizzle, and barely any dew. Could the summer of 1969, the man of the weather chart asked, be added to the other three of this century that were marked by the word "drought"?

It was still warm and dry the day Jim arrived, August 1st. Long before the plane from New York could possibly have landed, the kids and I were already at Schiphol Airport, tanned noses pushed against the glass door, looking for someone with a crew cut and a little tuft of hair on top of his forehead. "Whoever spots it first, Mom, should say so."

He'd be in his Brooks Brothers suit, I speculated, the brown one with the few strands of red. He wouldn't have taken the time to go home to change, God knew how long that man had been in the office in the past week. But the bed in Sini's house was now ready, so he could rest, and later, if there wasn't torrential rain, thunder, and wind "expected along the coast," we'd go to the boardwalk. Friday was fireworks night, and there'd be music in front of the merry-go-round. It would be like a scene in a poem he had jotted down years ago and put in a drawer:

> "A lot to do and wishing / it wasn't such a gray day and remembering / the fog over the river / There is always so much / work / but tonight we'll go to the park and / listen to the band / you and I."

The conveyor belt began to rotate, my kids raced forward, figures appeared, a single suitcase spinning around before it settled and slid around the curve, then more luggage, people starting to pick it up.

Jim walked sort of bent, I thought, and he looked drawn. The minute he saw us, though, he laughed, made funny faces at Kathy and Julie, whose arms were out too, "Daddy."

"My little girls," he shouted and then his special names for them, Russian-sounding, drawn from his ancestry perhaps. He lifted them up, hugged them, hugged me, and pressed us against him.

"Would you believe what my secretary asked when I was on my way out? 'Do you need anything to calm your nerves?' 'Gertrude,' I said, 'I'm not taking any sleeping pills, sedative, or whatever you're suggesting. I'm going to see my family.'"

Once more we trekked through Holland, the four of us now, with a map this time and a camera. "Stand still, girls, you too, Ann, a little longer," until the light was just right. And just as in New York, on Sunday afternoons when we went places, I walked behind him and the children, happily listening to talks about googolplex, a number so huge it was hard to comprehend; about anything, Atlas who would hold up the heavens with the mere strength of his head and hands, Jim said, but who held Atlas up? At times, as in New York, Jim would turn around, beaming, and say he loved me. When we stopped for something to drink, he'd draw animals, dragons, but not frightening-looking; nonsensical ones. He gave them names, too: "This is Zloop, but that one, with bigger toes and the tail not quite as pointed, we'll call Wlap."

How many fathers, my family asked, would read to their children at night, not just a page or two, and not with a face that said, "Is it that time again?" His whole body went into it, he even sang to them. Was what they heard like the Dutch lullaby "Sleep little one, outside there walks a sheep"? Yes, like that, and different. His was more direct, wishing the child a peaceful night. It's what his mother sang to him in the big house in Philadelphia. No, not only on vacation did he do all of this, at home too, no matter how late it got to be, and whether the kids were fully awake when he walked in or not.

And his Dutch was good, they always thought Americans could speak nothing but their own language, and badly at that, in mumbles. And what a pleasure to cook for him, he was so appreciative. We never saw anyone eat with such delight. Yes, he was the same at home: "I can't wait to see what's on the table, Ann," before he even hung up his coat.

At night, as we lay close in whoever's house we stayed, looking back on the day, he said my family made sitting around and talking about nothing in particular a cozy, happy climate, the kind his landlady, Madame Giraud, had created during his year in Paris. "Join me," she'd say when he returned from his classes at the university, "Come, *chou-chou*," or "big boy," as she had called the American soldiers when they came to liberate her country. "Here, take a chair," and they'd chat, the espresso pot between them. He even had Christmas dinner with her and her family as though he were her son, and was invited to a granddaughter's baptism. More than once, in this spare bed or that, he brought up Paris. "I want to go back there, Ann, and ring Madame Giraud's bell. I want to show her my wife."

I tensed up, I always did when he talked about travel. When I do get to Europe, I'd think, I only want to be in Holland, my family is small, getting more so all the time, who knows when the last visit will be?

"We can do it, Ann. The job's going well. I want to take you to the Tour d'Argent"—he once ate duck there—"Show you the cafés I hung out in, and the kiosk where I used to buy *Libération*, and the little store of my *béret de luxe* ... Shall we say the next time?" "I'll think about it," I promised, hoping that would settle it. Already we planned to take off for a few days, just Jim and me, which we hadn't done since our wedding, when the waitress at breakfast asked whether we were both on our honeymoon, looking at me when she said "both." But I hardly knew that man who kept squeezing my hand. I had only met him six or so times. Why did he talk so much, and quickly, and what about, history again? Gettysburg perhaps, it wasn't far from where we were, Split Rock in the Poconos, about sixty miles from where he grew up; this brand-new husband who, when sound asleep, had wandered about the room, arms out as if he were searching for someone who wasn't there and wasn't coming either. He kept going around and around, from the fireplace, embers still glowing in the dark, to the armchair by the window, where we had sat snugly away from the snowy landscape, naked, my face hidden against his chest. Who could remember what was said that morning after penetration, I was still worried, had I done my part right? Should I have groaned or grunted instead of meowing like a kitten, begging to be spared?

"The book you want me to write, Jim," I kept saying, curled up against him at night, at Sini's, at Rachel's, and in Winterswijk, "How do I know I can do it? At college—I didn't even go to a good school—I worked hard on a story, once, the life of an ant. I worked on it for a week and three extra days. "DUMB" got written on the title page, in red; "VERY DUMB" in fact. At Johan's and Dientje's, I never got a good mark from Sini either. It was either too condensed, 'What's your hurry, there's plenty of time,' or she'd tell me never to write about travels I hadn't made myself."

"This one," Jim said, comforting me as if I were a baby, stroking my face, kissing my eyelids, "Is your own story. You've lived it from beginning to end. Don't be in awe of schooling, it counts for a great deal less than you think. It gives you a base, like a pair of shoes. Still, it's up to you to walk. Write the way you speak, and you'll be fine. When you go to the Oostervelds with the kids, be sure to bring your list of questions, listen to what they say, and observe. You'll have a whole week to take notes. Once you're back in New York you write down everything, the bad as well as the good, whatever you remember. I'll read it, guide you, and pull you through." Whispering now, he said, "Make it solid, make it real, the way you yourself are. And it will last."

ON THE TWELFTH OF AUGUST, Jim and I went to Usselo in my stepmother's car. "Glad I don't have to go," she laughed. "Your father took me there once, that was plenty for me."

"Jule," Kathy warned, "When we go with Mom, don't eat that many plums again, remember the other year you sat in the outhouse all afternoon and cried?"

Julie had her own memories. "Tante Dientje will pick up my arm again, Kath, and tell Oom Johan, 'Feel for yourself, it weighs nothing. Her arms have waistlines, Kath, but I'm not allowed to say "fat," too close in language. "Mom," looking brighter already, "what's the Dutch word for 'rotund?'"

With a gift, a glass bowl I knew they'd love, one so heavy it made my legs buckle, we left for Usselo. It's not far from Winterswijk, perhaps forty kilometers. For the first ten or so, till the town of Groenlo, the road is straight and dark, bordered on both sides by oak trees, branches groping across to form a dome. I know, I biked there often enough. The sun hid behind haze that morning, darkening that ceiling even more. The leaves called up fall too, the green already looking dull here and there, the shade they turn before changing color completely.

I pointed it out to Jim. And again. Finally he saw. "Eh-huh." I babbled some more. "Is it always the same oaks that start this aging process, and if so, would the same ones also be the first to bud? Does it have to do with their position in the light?"

He nodded, barely. Strange, it wasn't like him not to talk, he loved trees, he could go into rapture over one, the way others glorified the stock market. When New York got hit with a lot of snow, Jim was the one who ran out of our building, broom in hand, to sweep the scrawny ginkgo in front so it wouldn't snap.

I bent closer to the windshield for yet another look at what edged the road. "I'm still wondering about those oaks, Jim, how much light they get ... stop me if you've had enough." He didn't. "Does it determine when leaves bloom and how soon they wither?" No answer. He sure wasn't talkative today.

He had been quiet all morning, around the kids too, but not like this. Maybe having to go back to New York was on his mind, I thought, or the pile of work that was bound to face him on Monday. "No," he said, "I don't mind working, you should know that."

I didn't press further, it wasn't done in his family. When before my wedding I asked his mother what kind of dress she had worn at hers, her eyes flashed as though I had done something terrible. Those matters are unimportant, she said, as when a cousin rang their doorbell once at three in the morning, upset, barefoot, her baby in her arms. "Come in," they said, "there's the couch, make yourself at home." She stayed for a week and was never asked why, nor why she had come in the first place.

"What's wrong, Jim?" It rolled out, whether it was prying or not.

He turned to me. He looked startled, as if I had caught him in something. "Nothing is wrong," he said, took my hand and held it, "Nothing to worry about." He did stammer some; that was not new or alarming, he sometimes did when he got agitated or nervous, or when something was on his mind and he wanted to get it out in a hurry. Only at his mother's funeral, when I expected this and kept thinking, please, let his tribute be over soon, he didn't stumble once; he even read a poem, Robert Frost's about two roads, and he was fine through all twenty lines. I counted them.

His silence probably has to do with going to the Oostervelds, I convinced myself, having to see for himself there was a time in my life when I had to hide. I wasn't eager to make that visit myself, I'd be so naked there. Would I have to show him where the chamber pot used to sit? With commentary perhaps? It wasn't always deep enough, Jim, especially when a half-dozen soldiers occupied the downstairs part of the house and Dientje could only empty it at night. About the enemy and that pisspot: If you're the first to use it, those sounds travel down. Can be heard. Can even kill. We put a pillow underneath to muffle the trickles during that time of billeting, which might have lasted no more than five weeks, but felt like a lifetime. I lost my voice from having only whispered. Even after the soldiers moved out again, I couldn't speak.

I imagined taking him through the house. All right, let's get bedtime over and done with. Here's where your wife's body was wedged, along with Johan and Dientje, in a space barely wide enough for two, and believe me, they were never thin people. And there, on the floor, was Sini's spot for sleeping, an awfully hot room it was, Jim, I don't know whose body gave off most heat. There's more. In the corner near the closet into which we crawled when danger seemed near stood the pail with sanitary napkins, Dientje's too, a merger of blood on strings of cloth waiting to be washed and shared all over again.

Let me walk ahead of you, I know the stairs that lead up there, sixteen steps, careful, those brass rods that are supposed to keep the runner, also red, adhered to the wood might slip out of their holes. On those steps, Jim, Sini "enlightened" me when I first needed to use one of those rags. She used a story that baffled, about fruits and bees, and seeds you needed to watch out for. That was enough past for now.

"Very little traffic today," I rattled, without checking whether it was so or not. Jim lifted my hand, pushed it against his cheek. "*Wifetje*," he said, with much feeling, and pronouncing it perfectly with three syllables as the Dutch would, the diminutive getting its very own *tje*.

"Dientje must already be stirring the soup, Jim."

"No, not with her finger. I hope?"

"For that, Jim, she uses a spoon. She'll want you to eat more than one plateful, 'Soup goes through thinly,' she'll say. 'It comes out the same way,' Johan will add, one leg already out the door, on the way to his tree." There, a reference to something urinary was made.

Never before, I continued, to myself now, had I brought a man to their house. Jim, even in his army fatigues and plaid sports shirt, looked unlike anyone they had wanted for me. Koos, was that his name? Who used to eat sand as a kid and had to wear cardboard tubes around his arms to stop him from swallowing another mouthful, but still walked with his elbows out? You'll change him, Annie, they said, or some other local, whose haircut made you think his neck went on forever, and with teeth, the few that were there, mossed over. Anyone at all so I could've been living next door, chasing goats. Or pigs, Usselo's fauna. On the topic of pigs, nothing's so bad as pig manure, Dientje was bound to announce. "Sniff for yourselves and tell me, bad, right?" I'd have to translate everything too, a few words of civilized Dutch, and they'd slip back into their dialect.

I turned around and got my sunglasses from the backseat, next to the camera and the extra roll of film to refresh my memory later. I put them on and raised the collar of my blouse, the latest thing in New York; it could easily be considered a dress as well. At least I looked sophisticated.

The town of Groenlo appeared, a few narrow streets, a tooting bus and out again, on to another road, foliated too and hinting at a different season. "At an intersection on the other side of this town, Jim, my father got killed. I'm sure I told you how he was on his way to a cattle market, as always wanting to be the first one there, when it was still so dark you couldn't distinguish one cow from another. He never slowed down, he bolted after a grocery truck, gambling that he too could still squeeze across." Stupid man.

"I'm glad we aren't on that road," Jim said softly. "It happened quickly, though, he wasn't hurting or struggling. That was was good. Ann," urgent now, "always remember that I love you."

Of course. I said something equally sweet, "same here," or some such, my love-yous didn't come out as easily as his.

With my arm around his shoulder we covered more road. I began to feel lighter, more at peace. A little to the east, or was it north, the haze was shrinking, and the trees were farther apart, forming a less oppressive landscape.

"Apparently, my father was very quiet the day before the accident, Jim, as if he sensed that something was going to happen. You think that's possible?"

"Maybe, and then again," cheerfully, "it could all have been imagination, his and of those who claimed they knew."

I felt better yet, it was turning into a good day after all. Even if you went to Usselo with four thoughts, none pleasant, they disappeared when you got closer and could practically already see the Oostervelds' door, dark green, that opened onto their kitchen, begonias on the sill, Johan looking out over them, for our car, "Any minute I expect them to be here, Dientje," who, in her best apron, would be waiting too.

"The weather again, I know, but look, more mist lifting off the tops of trees. You've been lucky, Jim, I've known it to be everything here in August, up to and including just right for mittens."

"It has been a great vacation," he said.

"*Sshht.* Not has been, there's tomorrow still, Jim, and four more days after that ..."

A few lazy sunrays lit up the road ahead. A horse neighed and a handful of geese in the meadow we drove by stepped back, synchronized as if to music. I thought of Father once more, and of the German ditty he'd sing through closed lips, "Don't wait, life is short." At least he had met Jim and liked him.

"Remember when we got married, the only Dutch you knew had to do with grass, the color of sky, and a bovine illness or two?—which surely would impress my father, I thought. But, no, 'Has Shim'—he always pronounced our last name wrong too, giving it a German twist—'Has this Shim of yours had any education to speak of? His conversation is so limited ...'"

We laughed. I rubbed my face against Jim's arm, like a kitten, or someone not quite grown up, maybe.

He stopped the car.

He needed a break? We had been driving—I looked at my watch—for only twenty-five minutes, "another fifteen and we'll be there, Jim."

"Not sick." He said it again, beginning to sound sharp, "And not coming down with anything either." He didn't know what was wrong, he had slept all right, he was just very tired.

"A few minutes out of the car and I'll be fine again."

He walked across the grassy verge, stretching his arms, shaking his feet, running some, up to the fourth tree and back along the ditch. He did seem fine, his color was good, and look at that energy now. I stopped being concerned. Such a sweet face, and so boyish still at thirty-seven; it had barely changed from when we met, in Boston, on a date arranged by a friend. He was finishing school, and I thought, how painterly, in a beret, not at all like a businessman-to-be. And he looked so poor, seemed to me, his jacket patched on both elbows, not even with corduroy that would at least have matched the rest, with leather yet, taken from who knew where, a pair of shoes? A case of borrowing from one to cover the other?

Much later, when it was all over, his life over, even later than that, I wondered whether on our way to my past, on that road to Usselo, Jim was seeing his own hamlet perhaps, the one he moved to when he was a kid. That summer, that vacation, and further back even, when he said, "Investigate your history, Ann," was he beginning to relive his? That particular day while I waited in my stepmother's car with a view of him, trees and on the other side of the ditch, fields, rye mowed, gathered and bound in sheaves, was he back in Lumberville?

He didn't know why they moved there, nor did his sister and brother. Because their mother loved nature? Because it was safer? Philadelphia was a port, in danger of being bombed; it was war—the same one I survived and perhaps Jim didn't. Or was life in the country healthier and cheaper—Bob was always short of funds—or was it the fine Quaker school that, Idy said, might give them scholarships, or because that little house on the canal was available for rent, the river right across the towpath, a setting for a book, a tale of adventure, a fortress from which to fight battles and control the seas, but where, when shortly after the unpacking was done, the bit of furniture that fit, all the books and Idy's drawings, whimsical and elfin, they were told the marriage was over. "Divorce," that's how they got it, straight. Not that there was someone else, a friend of the family. They had had no idea there was trouble; Bob had never been around much, he was a journalist who worked for a daily paper, he wrote all night and slept when they were up. Idy cried a lot, but that's the way she was, always excited about something or nervous or tense, an artistic temperament.

The marriage should not be unhappy, it couldn't be. Jim was born to rescue, conceived to bring back happiness, Idy told him. Was he on the side of the road going to Usselo, seeing not the tiny shed off in the distance, but that lockhouse that Bob still visited on weekends to see the children, but where on Mondays when the train took him away, Idy sobbed and didn't stop, not even after she had clutched the bunch of daisies Jim would pick for her?

Or was he, running to and fro between trees, what kind I forget, no longer seeing Lumberville when we met and both still lied; he said that his boyhood had been idyllic. A good place to grow up, with its pleasant haziness of Indian summer, the little hills and valleys in which to roam, the smell of good soil in the first few minutes of rain, autumn on the river sketched continuously by his mother, upriver scenes and downriver scenes. But was that other hamlet in front of his eyes, the one he had moved to just with her? The cat and dogs hadn't come either, no space, only for books, Jim's and his mother's, the art books and French books, her sketchbooks and *The Crock of Gold*, a fantasy story she liked so much that the author's name, James Stephens, became almost letter for letter Jim's first and middle name, James Steven.

Not a bad place either, he had said about that town and the house in which they lived in a couple of small rooms. Lovely shutters, the color of iodine, discernable even at night from the sill where he liked to sit. Ideal rooms for reading, he said, which they did a lot of, alone and to each other, and where he drew elaborate maps of the world, and where Idy taught him Russian learned from her mother. But in those rooms, within easy earshot of trains empty save for coal, she had been terrified. What if the landlord and his wife, they lived right underneath, were making fun of her? What if they were speaking of the noises her stomach made, the burps and hiccups? Were they loitering below her window again, wondering whether she was around, or peering at her through a pane? They are mad, she kept yelling—and writing it all down. They detest Jews; the landlord is on his way up the stairs, I can hear him with both sets of ears, he's coming up with a warrant to get me out, he'll want more money for these oversized closets, I can't pay more; no, I won't accept alimony, thank you, he'll ask me whether Bob divorced me or I him. I'm not a floozy.

After biking away from the same wonderful school he still went to and after having shopped for food so he could fix a meal for both of them, he never knew whether she'd be up there in those rooms, uncombed and unkempt, filling up her sketchbook with big blotchy flowers, headless dancers, closed umbrellas hooked along the backs of empty chairs. Was she sewing clowns onto a piece of canvas, or had she been too scared to stay in and was flitting about looking for him? But where? His schoolgrounds again? Behind a tree?

Jim was coming back to the car now, I saw.

I leaned out and called him over. "Jimmy," I asked, "Are you feeling any better?" He bent down to kiss me.

"Much," he said. "It's time to go on."

Part II

THIRTEEN DAYS LATER the phone call came, the day Kathy, Julie and I would have gone back to Usselo for the second visit.

The phone kept ringing. Who knew what hour it was, early dawn at most. In the bed next to mine the kids kept breathing deeply.

Why wasn't my stepmother getting up, one tiny sound, she always complained, "and my night is ruined." I pushed my head deeper into the pillow, trying to sleep some more too.

There, her door and padding sounds in the hall. The ringing stopped. Now I could doze off again.

"Annie." Whispered. "For you, I guess, America."

Kathy and Julie stirred, just a little.

Onto those hall tiles myself then. Some emergency? Over to the blanket chest where the phone sat. A crisis? "Jim?"

Phil, his brother, was on the line. He said something, a couple of words. They didn't hit. "Tell Jim I'm coming," I said, already looking at the door in the hall. "I'll leave immediately. Tell him that."

"It's too late," the voice answered, thin as a blade. "You do need to come to New York, though."

"Will you be there?" I asked.

"Back to Washington, on the first shuttle out," I heard, then the click. And overseas was just that again, a distant place.

The cold of the tiles, from Italy, with embedded leaves, snail shells, and possibly fossils as well, spread through my feet, and higher. With the receiver still pressed to an ear I raised my eyes toward the expensive-looking wall clock, a bluebird painted across the dial. Five o'clock. Was it still Sunday in New York, I should've asked Phil, or Monday already? Was I confused again about what time here, which hour there? As confused as I used to get with math problems that posed *A* is leaving home to meet *B* who is also on his way but left earlier or later along a road filled with obstacles or not, when will they meet?

I tried to think where I had been when it had happened. In Winterswijk, yes, but where exactly? Considering the six hours' difference and the fact that Jim had been dead for a while, it could have occurred, been done, while I was at the cemetery for a look at Father's tombstone. I hadn't wanted to go, but my stepmother insisted. "It's only proper, Annie, that when you come back for a visit you include him too."

I looked down again at her blanket chest, a Persian rug on top, a bowl with exotic fish, and the telephone, all of it illuminated by a lamp, Venetian or from Florence, with a light that seemed to stretch all the way across Holland, from Winterswijk to Sini's apartment, where Jim and I had slept the night before he left, in that room where he couldn't find anything when day came. He kept running around, which wasn't like him at all, looking for his wallet, passport, clothes, he couldn't find those either, and he was late. He snapped at me or he glowered, as if it was all my fault. Everything went wrong that morning of his departure. The suitcase wouldn't close, the lid all but broke when he forced it down with his foot, perhaps crushing the tile he was taking home, a present for his secretary, a pathetic tile I now saw, of a guy pushing a wheelbarrow far too big for him. And he still had to tie up the package containing the clay pot he was bringing back to friends. He had trouble, the string kept slipping off.

"Leave that damn pot," I said, "I'll bring it, they'll get it a few weeks later, so what?"

No, he didn't want to be taken to the airport, it would be silly, we'd see each other soon. "Go back to Winterswijk, Ann, to the kids." When I did put him on the KLM bus in the Hague, I insisted on seeing him off that far, he hurried aboard—barely waving back.

I wrote to him immediately, the minute I got back to Sini's apartment; I couldn't get him out of my mind. Was the trip all right, Jim? The office in good shape? Are you having fun? Don't forget to call Lloyd and Dottie, and have you let Carole and Vinny know you're back? Had your dinner with Pat yet? Will you make sure to make plans for Labor Day? As he had said he would.

After I heard from him, a letter as cheery as could be, written right away too, I told myself, *You always worry over nothing,* his odd behavior the morning he left. And the few days before. Wasn't he allowed? "It wasn't my day," he wrote. "That pot that wouldn't stay tied ... it never made it home ..."

Quietly I moved the receiver away from my face. That phrase Phil had used, *self-inflicted,* could it also have another meaning, one not so harsh? Self-respect, self-made, those were all good words. I should look it up, verify. In what, though? Why wasn't there an English dictionary in this place that had everything? Didn't every decent house have at least one? Where would you check, though? Under *self* or under *inflicted*?

"Annie," my stepmother was saying. Was she speaking to me?

I stared at her. "Suicide," I scraped out.

"My God," she said. "Last week when he was here he was fine." Her eyes were so big they frightened me. "*Sshht,*" she threatened, as if she expected me to add another word, or say the same one again. "*Ssssshht,* not so loud. The children ..."

I could hear them thumping over in their pajamas.

"What's the matter," they asked, looking serious. "Why aren't you still in bed?"

Their eyes ... just like his, brown and full of life.

I swallowed. Did Julie resemble him a little more than Kathy did? My stepmother was right, they shouldn't have to know the truth, they were so young, how could they understand?

"Daddy died. Of a heart attack."

They asked no questions, made no comment.

I took their hands and went back into the guestroom where up till, what, an hour ago?—Half a lifetime?—Kathy, Julie, and I had been peacefully asleep. I closed the door and got into the bed they shared.

I held them.

So cold, all three of us, we couldn't stop shivering. Or was it my body that did all the shaking?

I got up, took a blanket off my bed, returned.

Another one, maybe that would help.

Through the curtain a hint of gray began to show. I wondered if it was foggy. Had last night's wind, it had been so fierce, ripped off many leaves, had they stuck where they dropped? Or had they affixed themselves to something else wet? By noon I was supposed to be at the Oostervelds ...

From the railroad crossing down the road, the sound of the alarm clanked. Soon the first train would pull out of the station and pass. Already I could hear a whistle and the crunching of wheels. Holding my kids tight—could they even breathe?—I listened until the sounds faded and the crossing barrier lifted again.

"Mommy." Julie's voice from safely inside my arm.

"What, *poesje*?"

"Who'll take care of us now?"

"Kathy and I will," I answered, correcting myself right away. "Mommy will, of course, of the two of you."

I hoped Kathy would remember only that.

LATER—HOW MUCH LATER?—after the children had gotten dressed, chatting away as if nothing had happened, and had been summoned to the bathroom by my stepmother, "*Kom es hier, meisjes,*" and had gone over for the good-morning kiss, routine too, after staring at her (she wore nothing above her corset), and after they had come out, presumably tugging at their own nipples again and wondering whether anything as large as what Oma had could possibly come from anything so little, and when I heard them move around the kitchen, I too got up.

So cold again, or still cold, I put a shawl over my night-gown. A sweater then, as well. I couldn't stop shaking. My coat, too, yes. I snatched it off the rack in the hall and slipped back into the room; I wandered around, straightening a sheet, picking clothing off a chair, shouldn't I be doing something more with it? Into the laundry maybe? I put it down again.

I opened the curtain, my eyes bored through the window. The currant and gooseberry bushes were picked clean, the last batch having been turned into jam yesterday, two jars standing ready to come home with me.

Everything outside looked flattened, wet. Fall was near, the sky thick, the kind that made Jim call me from the office, "Put galoshes on the kids, Ann, and take the umbrella when you go out." So caring, I thought. What had he taken me for all those years of marriage, eleven almost, with an "I love you" for each day? As if I couldn't have seen for myself when rain gear was needed.

Behind the strip of sopping yard and gaunt bushes, the meadow in the back and the railroad crossing, was the slaughterhouse. On Tuesday the trucks would arrive again filled with calves, bleating and whimpering before they even got there. The same day of the week, almost thirty years before, Jews got swept into trains and across the border, ninety-three trains, in the dark, as now.

Why had Jim not called when he felt that bad; he knew how to pick up the phone. When I was here when Father died, he called twice in one week, Was I all right, did I need to stay longer?

Stay longer ... home is where I should have been, or should have followed him to the day after he had left; I knew something was off. Had I not been trying to write about "then," a time I should have left where it was, six feet under. Had I not been trying to figure out what was important enough to be brought back to life, and who?

I held my breath, standing motionless, the coat pulled around me as tightly as I could, last fall's purchase. Jule, Kath, come, we'll all go and help Mom pick out a coat, don't look at the price, Ann, get something beautiful.

If he stood in front of me now I'd beat him, shake him, pummel him with my fists, scratch his skin open like some ferocious animal, bite. Stupid, I'd spit out, idiot, you with your whatever, phi cum laudes, all I see is waste.

From the windowsill in front of me I lifted the spiral notebook, pages numbered one through eighty, questions for Johan on the left, spaces for answers on the right, just as Jim had suggested.

I flung it down. There, that's what I thought of his big ideas. Yells wanted to come out, raw cries held back. A puppy sound managed to escape. That's it, Annie, calling myself by my Dutch name, have you forgotten what sounds can do? Draw attention to people who'll come and kill. *Sshht*, your little girls are only a few walls away, you'll frighten them, keep yourself in check, you can do it, remember what Johan used to say? "Annie's a plucky kid, never a peep out of 'r, that one never even cried. Sini was the moody one and got depressed a lot. Let's face it, she was a lot older, hiding was harder on her, kids get used to things, she got a different nature too, our Annie 'preciates what I do, and why not, she's got a great life here ..."

"Johan," I whispered, hands against my throat to prevent any more sounds from coming out. "Even your chickens ran free."

If ever I got back to Holland, and who'd want to after this, but *if*, I'd skip Usselo. I could stay grateful without seeing Johan again, that squelcher of voice, that crusher of gut. The war's over. "Once an episode ends," Sini always says, "You go on to other things."

Who knew what Johan did to Jim, what damage he caused during our visit? Saved two people, ha-ha; caused one to die. It had something to do with it, if not everything.

I swallowed, suddenly feeling nauseated. That hotel in Amsterdam, ten guilders a night for a quiet stay, the folder said. The entrance was nice, no taking that back, geraniums, red, in boxes on either side of the main door, welcome-mat. A long staircase to the first floor but the distance to the bathroom almost nothing from where we had stayed in room number 3, where Jim ... no, I didn't want to go there yet. But had our door opened with a knob or not? And would it have made a difference? When had it been, anyway, before or after our outing to Zeeland, the province in the south of Holland we went to in a little airplane? I didn't look down, Jim did, at how the miles of water that had caused the flood of 1953 were being dammed in and he ... I was getting it all mixed up, plane, Amsterdam hotel that was to have been better than our honeymoon and the train ride; that I surely couldn't think about yet. But after the visit to Usselo. That's when the strangeness started. Or got worse. And stuck.

Johan was waiting by the gate, yelling something to bring out the townsfolk, "I'll be damned, here comes America to take a look. This here is the house, all right." But no one on the road opened the door, no window got raised, none of the neighbors stuck a head out, to be impressed. Only Dientje ventured over to the car, dentures in hand. "I can't talk with 'm, Annie, they clack, they're only good for eating. I got curls too, you notice? I said to the hairdresser, 'Make me pretty, I got an important day coming up.' You like the color?" Rusty, barbed-wire red as Sini's and mine had been during the war. "Stop it, woman," Johan shouted, "Yim here doesn't want to know what you got in the mouth or what sits on your head, he came for something else, I bet. In this house," swinging out an arm, "Our Annie hid out when she was a kid and these here," slapping himself on the chest, "Are the people that saved 'r. Yep, Yim," more drumming and voice trumpeting across fields and roads, across towns and oceans, "I'm the man who pulled it off."

We went in. I quickly checked the kitchen. Had anything changed? No, stone floor, stove going, coffee boiling away, four chairs around the table, one still with Opoe's cushion, a raised pattern of lumpy squares, rough horsehair, it always made me wonder how she could be comfortable on top of it.

In the good room everything was as it should be too, fake velvet tablecloth, the big chest along the wall, yes-yes, with family portraits, all yellowed except for Sini's and mine. Jim looked with great interest, who's this, who's that? As always the radio was unplugged, in case of lightning, right, Johan? Something was different, though. No flypaper hung from the ceiling.

"*Ja*, Yim," Johan beamed, "Annie notices everything. Those strips weren't right, that was a torturous death, such wrigglings were going on. Sometimes we even got stuck on 'm ourselves, it took an awful lot of pulling to get the hairs loose and let's face it, Dientje here already hasn't got that many."

She continued to trail about, fly-swatter held ready.

"Tell Yim to pull up a chair, Annie, here, near me, so he can hear everything. You too, get close, considering the fellow doesn't know what I'm saying. Stop the chasing, woman, our visitor"—now Dientje glanced at Jim—"Will think you're a retard or something. Is that what you want 'm to say when he goes home? Go get the cookie tin, show 'm what the baker here has knocked together. Usselo may not be as big as where you live, Yim, but we sure know what tastes good, there's so much butter in these there's no need to chew. Was different in the war, Annie, right? You should've seen 'r scramble up my lap, Yim, one-two-three and there she'd sit again, I couldn't keep 'r off it. *Ja,* comes an end to everything, that's how it goes. Hours, days, months, years, slip away with shadow's speed. Yim doesn't know but that's what people sing about here on New Year's Eve. Ma said it better, 'No point in buying more than one loaf of bread, we may not be around for tomorrow's slice...' I, for me, prefer Goddammit, says it all. I'll be damned, Annie has a husband. *Ja,* Yim, we never saw you before, makes you deaf to the fact she's married. He's not a bad-looking man, Annie, that I got to admit, no complaints there. I bet he can't wait to know how I managed to keep you alive. I'll tell him everything, don't worry, I'll unwrap it all."

He was slow in getting started, though, as if he was afraid that once he did, and finished, his day would be over.

I secretly noticed that the sky had completely cleared, pleasant weather for driving back, which we should be doing before too long, before the mist returned and glued itself back to the car and words or silence had nowhere to go.

"You're in no hurry to leave, *wa?* It stays light awfully long, you got time, and time it takes to tell about those years. Just about three, that's how many years the girls were here. Does something to you, Yim. For money, believe me, I didn't do it. Official honor I never got either, no medal from the government, nothing. Doesn't bother me, having gotten the girls through's what counts."

"That Mr. Hannink was clever, Johan, getting rid of 'm almost as soon as he took 'm in," Dientje laughed. "'It's only for two weeks,' he told us, the liar, and he never came back to get 'm."

"Why should he have, woman, he knew I could do it. 'No one else in Usselo but you, Johan, do I trust,' he said when he dropped 'm off. Late at night, Yim, you should have seen 'm rattle, like leaves in October, and Annie here, so little, how could I have let 'r get dragged off to a death camp? Those girls needed me, that's why I did it. Sure, it was dangerous, Yim, you're Goddam right, plenty dangerous, could've done us all in, me, Ma, Dientje here. It took a lot of courage to do what I did."

Quickly, Dientje took her teeth out again. "Don't forget Mr. Hannink was our landlord, Johan, was hard to say no to 'm, 'specially with the low rent he charged."

"Had nothing to do with it, woman, he never did anything to this dump, it's got the same paint on it for forty-eight years, an outhouse and no running water, what're you thinking about, me? Afraid of Mr. Hannink? It's afterward that it hits you, Yim, then you see how risky it was. But I'd do it again, I'll be damned if it isn't so. Dientje here was scared, admit it, woman." She admitted to nothing, too busy glaring up at the ceiling where two flies were copulating.

"Not me, Yim, I wasn't even scared when we had the military staying here too. I wish you could've seen 'm, rifles dangling from their necks, medals on the collar big as pancakes. 'Do we leave now?' Annie asked. The look on 'r face, Yim, I can hardly say it, of death. 'I'm not putting you out in the street,' I said. You know Johan won't let anything happen to you.' It was fine, Yim, no bother, nothing. Exciting, I'd say, Germans and Jews in the same house, who else would've dared? No one, right? Lemme tell you about one morning. Dientje, before I get into this story, shake some more of that stuff you call coffee out of the pot. *Ja*, Yim, as long as the cups aren't upside-down on the saucer we keep on drinking. Another cookie too, c'mon, woman, hurry up, it'll put some fat on their bones. This one morning, Yim, it was November 1944, no shortcuts, Annie, I want to make sure he gets every word I'm about to let go of. That morning, Yim, what a mess, Annie here comes downstairs in her pajamas and bumps into an officer. I'm not kidding, in the kitchen, that's where. 'I thought you had no children,' the fellow says. *Ja*, Yim, with German I have no trouble. 'Who is that girl, then?' Anyone else would've dropped to the floor with fright, not me. Soon as I could I ran to the stable to tell Dientje what happened. 'Stop sniveling,' I said to 'r. 'A different kind of action is needed. Get on your bike and say to your sister, we wanna borrow her kid for a day.' I figured he only saw Annie for a second, he won't know the difference between her and Rikie. I practically had to push Dientje on the bike, Yim, she kept wailing, but what if, what if. 'Had the Lord said that,' I told 'r, 'there would've been no world.'

"Annie here too thought the end had come, she was sitting upstairs in her jacket, waiting to be deported. D'you think Johan will allow that? I said to 'r. I would've dug the manure fork into 'm had he taken 'r away, I would've stopped at nothing, Yim, I swear. I never even went into the air-raid shelter, I built one by the walnut tree, I'll show you exactly where, don't worry. When the bombers came, they never saw me in there, Annie trembled so, how could I have left 'r in the house and saved myself? As soon as those planes came over I'd throw my body on top of 'r, protected her with my own flesh."

What went on in Jim's mind as he sat and listened, sitting very still, head tilted, not saying a word, his arm around the back of my chair? Where did he wander during my translation of Johan's epic? What distance did he take himself while

Johan and I kept up our duet, in perfect sync, my voice rising with his? "In times of trouble, Yim, that's when you find
out who's wheat and who's chaff."

He must have been thinking about something in his life.
What point did he plunge into? Perhaps before he was even
born? To resuscitate a marriage, his mother confided. Or at
her descent into madness, another rescue effort—failed.

Still standing in my stepmother's guest room, I stared down
at hands that looked cold and unfamiliar. Were they mine?
I spread out fingers, ten, stubby sort of, one with a wedding
band. I remembered what I ought to be doing, go home,
something there wasn't right. Was I hearing the phone again?
That's where I should be headed, to the phone, get a ticket,
proper documents, quick. Shoes, where were they? Couldn't
step back into the hall without them, those tiles stung. Hurry,
can't make officials wait or punishment will follow. Was that
them now? Speaking the language of police? One more second and I'd be marched off, where to, you could only guess.

From the same spot where I had remained all this time,
I saw it was raining. I looked out again at dripping bushes
and sopping wet grass. And so dark still, would it never lift?
You could almost imagine the sound of a foghorn, I heard
one the evening before I emi-immigrated—I did both, didn't
I?—when Father took me to see *Long Day's Journey Into
Night*, in Dutch, as a farewell and all I took in, none of the
words, only the foghorn and water that I heard cascading
down some window, growing in width and depth to an ocean,
such as I was about to be on.

Something began to seep back in, I'd be expected to cross
the ocean today too ... call an airline? Now? No, get more
clothes on, that first, you never knew where you would end

up, in what cold place, or what kind of defense was needed.
Even telephones could be dangerous. Such a bombardment
of thoughts today, newtimeoldtime, all shoved together, shat-
tering whatever sanity remained. I no longer knew who to
believe, what to do. Hide? But where?

I bent down, picked the spiral notebook with questions
for Johan, pages one through eighty, off the ground and put
it back on the windowsill, next to the piece of paper with
Jim's calculations of how far it was to Usselo in kilometers,
crossed out and replaced by miles so he'd feel in his bones
how long the drive to the Oostervelds' would take. The longer we were there, the more they said they had done, the
harder it became ...

Tense, wordless, feet deadened by Johan's bravery, Jim and
I worked our way up the stairs onto the landing, which was
dressed by an extra piece of red runner, and into the winter
room, called that because it could hold a stove.

I could keep my eyes closed and not bump into anything,
bed, washstand, and the window, covered by ivy now, giving
it the same color as the ceiling and walls, the green paint
broken only by the picture Opoe gave me to color in, a shepherd, five sheep, clouds overhead that I made beige, I had no
blue, and applied to the outline of two birds, wings reaching
toward the edge. "Teach me how to be Your child," the text
read, "Take me into Your fold, small as I may be."

We walked into the summer room. Automatically I began
to count, thirty boards one way, thirty the other, each board
twice the width of my hand. "If you look through the left
window, Jim, around and past the linden tree that I thought
of as mine, the way other kids would say, That's my bike, or
my route to school, you can see—I know about the cracks

in the glass, same three still there—just look over them and between the branches, see? You can spot some sky and the stable where Johan and Sini, at night, tended to the cows." And to each other, perhaps—but that only to myself.

Silently, we went back, from summer room to winter room, with the hole in the back of the closet, for when additional shelter was needed. Jim took a glimpse, shut the door.

And again to where, during the day, your eyes could follow the path Johan's and Sini's feet were on after dark, on their way to a place from which only the sound of cows escaped. And back over to the other room, where the birds on the Sunday-school picture were still stranded between the clouds and where the monthly rags still seemed to be poking out of a pail in the corner.

I sat down on the edge of the bed. Something clawed its way up, a wildness rose, something close to violence. I wanted to rip off my clothes, the blouse from New York that could easily be a dress, tear Jim's clothes off as well. I need you, my eyes begged, sit with me at least, right here on this mattress where for a thousand nights I pretended to be dead. I listened. No footsteps were coming up the stairs, no sound at all could be heard, Johan and Dientje must be in the kitchen. For a second, fear came back up, a soldier could be in there as on that morning when I had ventured down ... My eyes kept pleading with Jim to extinguish other people's heat that I'd been carrying around ever since the war. Feel me, even through my clothes you can tell my body will warm us both. Be a child with me, a time not so far in the past that we don't remember. I stuck out my arms. He didn't notice, he saw nothing of what I was thinking. His eyes were closed. His back pushed against the closet door, hiding the hole I used to crawl into during nightly raids when danger was imminent. He stood there, clamped against that door, appearing undone. As I was now.

From the hall came my stepmother's voice. She was on the telephone, talking to her daughter. "Yes, only thirty-seven years old, Nel. And in such good shape, you saw yourself when you met him, wasn't he trim? No, no history of heart trouble in his family that I know of. Quite a blow for Annie and the children, what d'you think?"

I lied to Kathy and Julie ... how could I have done that ... what if they ever found out from someone else? They'd never believe me again, think I lied about everything.

Jim's brother Phil, Jim's father, his wife, Phil's wife, Jim's sister, her husband. Would I have to ask all of them to lie too?

Again my stepmother's voice, again saying the same. How many more times did I have to listen to his age, "You're right, so young. No, no warning, no, just like that. He was quite an appearance, I want you to know, in his blue shirt and suit, quite elegant. His poor father. ... of course I met him, when Annie got married he was there too. Yes, devastated, I'm sure..."

Lying wasn't like me, not if I could help it. Your forehead shows anyway, Mother always said, a cross forms for everyone to see.

I couldn't stop shaking ... how could I face my kids? I had to, they were calling, from the kitchen, in Dutch, Oma, Mommie, *ontbijt is klaar*. Breakfast was ready.

COAT BUTTONED, suitcase next to me, I waited in the hall for the doorbell to ring but the car, courtesy of my step-sister and her husband, had not yet arrived. It was getting late, ten-thirty already and with Monday-morning traffic and all that rain it could easily take three hours to get to the air-port. Ten-thirty-one, another minute lost. What if I arrived when the plane had already taken off? It had been almost impossible to find a seat. KLM had none. It was still tour-ist season, they said, I couldn't expect to get what I wanted on the day I wanted. I didn't want ... if I could wait until tomorrow, maybe something could be done. Voice cracking and shivering so I could hardly form a word: "Wait? What if my husband were dying and needed to see me, doesn't your airline save a seat just for that? How dare you not think of an emergency, am I the first one?" Pan Am understood too. They offered condolences; that's how sorry they were. "Not even in the cockpit?" I screamed. "I'm small, I don't need a seat, I can stand."

There was only one more airline that flew to New York. Slowly I dialed, afraid of what the answer might be. If yes, I didn't have enough money; even if I did figure out how to charge something, I couldn't, the card was in Jim's wallet; same with the checkbook, that, too, was sitting in New York. I dropped the phone, ran to my stepmother, explained. She offered the money, didn't even want it back, a gift. Couldn't think of that now, I'd cry. EL AL had room, for more than one. No, no child would accompany me, I couldn't take them, who knew what I would find? They'd only come as far as Schiphol Airport. The other seat was for Sini. Johan told her to come. "We can't let our Annie make this trip alone. You go, Sini, you speak English." Or he would have come with me himself.

The alarming feeling in my throat was coming back. Each time someone does something nice for me today I want to cry. That's not what a person-in-hiding does, show more than is safe. Do what you used to, I told myself, when sounds could betray. Breathe deeply. Yes, like that, mouth wide open. It helps, doesn't it? If only my teeth would obey and stop rattling, like machine guns you can't see, the same staccato sounds that came from the package Jim wrapped the day he left, the clay pot that wouldn't stand still, defying the string and his hands that were trying to stuff it inside the paper into which it was supposed to fit. The time he put our bookcase together and it wouldn't go as easily as the manual said, with a minimum of experience you shall succeed, he had been upset too and shouted—into the room, not at me. Was that the telephone again, clanging away? What right do you have to keep upsetting me, I'm not home, wherever home is or has been, I'll never be home again, especially not at night. Those teeth, *shht*, do I need to warn you about the dangers inherent in your mouth? Clench them, tight as you can. Or I'll have you yanked out, that'll teach me to be quiet. Now also make fists. Of course you remember the extra safety measure. You probably thought after the war was over you could do away with all of that. Now you see. Next, push fingers so hard into the palms of your hands that you feel nothing, except pain you can control.

Ten-thirty-three. From how far away did that limo have to come? Sure, rain, Monday, traffic jams; an accident or two; red lights. At this rate I could easily be standing here a year from now, followed by another, one more, and part of a third; roots sprouting from my feet. I kept my eyes on the strips of knobbly glass in the hall door but nothing showed up yet, no contour of a parked car and no person walking up to the bell.

Sini would have to know about this suicide. I'd better not even think the word. Or it might slip out no matter where you were or with whom. Best to hammer-hammer the other cause of death into my head, so when anyone asks, "Of what?" the heart attack will come out naturally. If you could master the cleaning lady's name at the age of seven months, Aadje, not even an easy word, you can surely do this, heart-ack, see? Almost right, like letting out a sigh.

If Johan knew the truth, would he think it was my fault? That I'd had a hand in it? And see me in a new light, smudged?

I'm not a killer, I didn't do it, don't point your finger at me, I've never even seen Christ.

Where am I? In which street in Winterswijk? Near the Catholic school? "Killer," kids are yelling. "You had it coming." Tomatoes that splash when they land, chunks of red, dripping. I'm not running alone, I have a little boy by the hand I'm in charge of. "Move your legs, Brammetje," I whisper, "They're almost here ..." What happened to him? On what train did he end up? Which Tuesday?

It was hard to get Jim's kind of death out of my head. Jews sometimes did that during the war, commit suicide rather than be slaughtered. And before the war, I heard about two others, the cantor who sang like an angel of the Lord but who was also the treasurer of the synagogue, and got caught taking. And there was an aunt, especially hush-hush ... her husband drove her to it, they said.

I thought my marriage was good. Sure, there was some nagging going on, isn't there something less than ideal in everyone's? Does that make a person go out and kill himself? Why didn't he divorce me? That wasn't unheard of in his family ...

The gall of that telephone, clattering away again, get out of my ears and the back of my head or I'll have to do something, pull out the wire, shut it up for good. Was it Jim, maybe? To say he was having a good day after the bad night? For a second I strained my ears. Then I crossed the hall again, suitcase in hand, increasing speed when I got closer to the door. I stopped pacing, stared at the pocketbook that seemed to be dangling from a fist. Jim had given it to me for my birthday this past spring, dinner out by candlelight, when we talked about the book and he said, "You gave me the best years of my life, Ann." Did he know then, five months back, that it was going to end? I clapped a hand against my mouth, muzzling what threatened to come from there. Of course there had to be a gestation period. You wouldn't finish a meal, wipe your chin on your napkin, push the chair back, and then ...

Where was he now? That, Phil hadn't said.

I went back over this morning, *no, not* the phone-call, I knew what it said, but over a second letter that had come.

I'd biked over to the post office to get it. Look for something blue, I said to the man at the window, an aerogram, "Human Rights" printed on the top, right above "US postage, 13 cents." Yes, details, I know, but everything about these letters is important. Nothing? Please go through the bag again, or check in the back for a letter addressed to Reiss, care of de Leeuw, the daughter of that car crash, you're right, three years come October.

It had been written on the same day as the first letter, only late at night, five days before his death, another "Dearest wife" and "All's fine"; a wonderful weekend in store, Ruth and Sam had invited him to the country, Lake Celeste—he must not have gotten there—and there was a note for the children, "*Kinderen,* when you return we shall speak Dutch each day at home." Who did he mean by *we*? I charged toward the door again. Right, I had to wait for the car. I tried to picture Jim when he'd written that letter, at the dining room table? Cat on his lap? Who knew, nothing could be trusted anymore. A newspaper underneath the typewriter so it wouldn't mar the table? His sister's, she gave it to us when she and her husband decided to live on a boat.

At first I couldn't see him, only a hand, the left one with the birthmark, that was all, nothing else. There, a mouth came through, no lips, just a line that wouldn't open, a bristly tuft of hair brushed as thoroughly as though an entire forest had to be tamed, a shiny shoe, a dimple. But the pieces wouldn't connect. Maybe if I concentrated harder, got him out of that room, pictured him in another one, walking or standing or lying down ... but all that showed, no matter where I imagined him, was something that had no real shape, only a loneliness I couldn't touch.

What if a third letter was on the way, written on the very

night of his death and my kids got hold of it? I'd need to warn my stepmother not to let them near it. Make it disappear until I return.

I opened my bag, gingerly, looking around while unclasping it, it was so easy to transgress and not even know you were doing it. Good, both letters received since he left were with me, some proof that he had given us, me, a thought when he still could. I fished out the brochure of where we had stayed for our one night of freedom away from my family with no kids, a replay of our honeymoon, we said, but better, we knew each other more. QUIET HOTEL, I read. INN. MANOR. My God, they wanted to be everything, one-stop for all your happiness, even within walking distance from the station. I opened the leaflet and looked at the pictures on page two, the breakfast room, low-hanging lamps suspended between beams; the reception area where, right alongside the keys, they displayed souvenirs you could buy, windmills, dolls in the lace-cap-and-wooden-shoes costume; and postcards of Amsterdam by night. The picture of the bedroom was small, as if it didn't matter, as though bedrooms were of no importance, not even an entire bed was shown and no door. The checked bedspread that they wanted you to see, a shade of calming beige matching that of the curtain, and the seating arrangement near the window, a low rattan table and two chairs. And the bedside lamp, with a tiny shade on a tall pole bent at an angle—"the way de Gaulle walks, Jim, his head trying to keep up with his feet." He didn't seem to like my sort of joke.

"It isn't all he embodies, Ann. He's also an honest man who still sees himself as the savior of France."

That entire room could have been the one we stayed in, with a view of the canal, cars parked so close to the edge; it was a miracle they weren't falling in. "Even if I did know how to drive, Jim, I'd never park there, one gust of wind or your foot brushing the wrong pedal ..."

Bare feet resting in each other's lap, we talked, Jim doing most of it. Not scary at all, our lease was about to expire, should we renew for three years, or less; where to go for next year's vacation, Block Island? The *New York Times* recently had an article about it, calling it an unspoiled place. "That sounds great, Jim." Once he got back home he'd look into it, maybe we could rent a cottage again, as we had on Shelter Island and on Fire Island the year before that.

We stayed silent for a while. "The apartment will feel empty, Ann, without you and the kids." We counted in how many days we'd join him, nineteen, actually less, he'd be at the airport halfway through the nineteenth to pick us up. "Let's stop counting, Jim, that makes it sound like too many days, let's say before you know it we'll be back." A boat went by, festively lit, accordion music drifted up and in through the window, disjointed chords, someone practicing? And I heard shouting, something I was surely wrong about, as Jim was talking quietly. I must have been imagining it, I had been nervous all day; I could easily be hearing undertones that weren't there at all. As on the first night we ever spent under the same roof, way before our honeymoon, when I went to visit him in Detroit where he put me up in a room next to his and I was convinced I heard footsteps, his no doubt, wanting to come in and do more than hold me fully dressed. Right by my door I heard them. Any minute and it'll spring open, I thought. Lock it, I told myself, but what if he could hear me do it, he'd think I didn't trust ...

For some reason or none at all, sitting by the hotel window, the stretch of canal I could see got transformed into something bigger, a vision of Jim in the swimming pool of his favorite school, he the only one in it, hands on the concrete edge and beaming. There was a snapshot of that somewhere, in a drawer.

It was still early when we closed the curtain. We started to make love. Nothing happened, nothing celebratory to mark our night alone. "After how many years, Ann?" We joked about it, we must've forgotten how in the beds of my relatives. I even quoted the few words I remembered about Passover, "Why is this night different?" We didn't know, we said, but there was still tomorrow morning, if not before. We kissed and turned over.

I waited for sleep to come. Jim seemed to have succeeded, he was lying very still and breathing peacefully. I kept turning over, back, side, on my back again, muscles as tense as before. You'd think that after all the running around we had done today I'd be too limp to make another move. Into one restaurant and out, some too small, or too cramped, too narrow, too whatever, the ceiling so low it threatened to crunch. And on we trekked, next to canals we had probably been on before, main canals, canals that ran crosswise, and canals that, way back, had been filled in.

I wondered if I should get up and sit by the window, try to unwind. I raised myself on an elbow, lowered my feet to the side of the bed, rejected the idea and lay down again, careful not to wake him. With my eyes wide open I looked at the curtain, still beige. A shade darker perhaps? And was that the moon beginning to peek through? A passing car threw a yellow reflection on the wall, it spread and disappeared. Maybe I was beyond tired and needed to be patient just a little longer, picture something calming to end this day, something to follow all the I-love-yous, which had come over and over again.

Along which canal had I tried to wriggle loose, away from

his arms, and those words. "What's wrong, Jim?" I began to look over my shoulder for something to divert him, anything, a dog holding its own leash, or a pair of clogs on some villager in town for the day. Even after I talked him out of a leather jacket he wanted—"It's not for the office, Jim, and once back in New York how often will you get to wear it?" He kept repeating the I-love-yous.

"If anything ever happens to me, Ann, remember only that—my love."

I must have fallen asleep after all, but who knew for how long? Jim was stirring too. We moved toward each other, tentative at first, joyful then. It made me very happy, something at least was normal again. Wait, Jim, not yet, I need to get ready. I slid out of bed, grabbed something to wear and headed straight into the hall. A single bulb at the end lit my way, twenty steps at most. It took no time to come back, two minutes or less, but a different person was waiting for me and not where I expected him, right behind the door, he always did that, and together we'd make the trip back to bed, already skin next to skin. The curtain was open. Not the window too? We'd be eaten up by mosquitoes so close to the canal. I stepped farther into the room. He was dressed, that too made no sense, in his T-shirt and shorts, and standing next to the bed, holding that lamp that earlier had reminded me of General de Gaulle. His hands were clasped around the pole, which seemed more atilt than before, he had lifted it off the ground as though he was taking it somewhere. He stood like a medieval warrior bound for service on the city walls. We had seen something like that, just this afternoon, *The Nightwatch*, at the Rijksmuseum.

"It's me, Jim," I said. "It's Ann. It's your wife."

His voice shook something into the room. I wasn't sure what. Key? It's in my hand, Jim. Had he thought I'd lost it?

Sini always accused me of that. If it isn't your wallet it's your bag, and if it isn't that it's your keys. Now you lost your husband too, she'd say.

"What made you take it, Ann?"

The key, yes, "I didn't want someone wandering in, you were in bed when I left, you were naked."

"Exactly the point," he said, in that same eerie voice.

A corner of the moon blinked back.

"You of all people, Ann, should know how it feels to have a door closed on you, leaving you without a way to get out. How could you have taken the key? And left me, locked up."

"Here," I said, faintly, "take it."

I put the key on the bed. And picked it up again. "On the table it goes." He still made no move.

"I know what to do, I'll put it back in the door, look, Jim, done, all fixed"—treating him like a child.

I should have put the key in his hand, that might have solved it, instead of standing there telling him I'd meant no harm, that I'd had no idea it would upset him. I should have asked what he feared, of course, who he thought would attack or what he had heard or seen. What muffled voices? Whose faces?

Blotting out the hotel room, I imagine another room, at a different time and place. A boy, it had to have been Jim —thirteen? fourteen? fifteen?—is sitting on the windowsill, the sides framed by shutters the color of iodine. It's a good place to wait, you can hear trains as they approach, some piled high with coal, others bringing passengers, his father perhaps.

His listens sharply, one comes roaring closer, might it be the one that Dad is on? Behind him, inside the apartment, his mother listens too, with the double set of ears she claims to have.

"The noise is starting again," she shouts over the din,

"The landlord and his horrid wife are back. They're on their way up to the apartment with their extraordinary ideas. 'Are you divorced?' they ask a hundred times a day. You're a good boy, James. Tell them I don't want them in here. They frighten me, they're nasty, they'll say I did it, they'll want to fight, I heard them whisper, 'Why don't we get the creature?' I made no fun of them, they are crazy, 'We detest Jews,' they'll say it until I'm almost crazy too. Stop them, James, they are ringing our bell ..."

Still waiting for the car, I scowled at the hall door again—no change—and at the hotel brochure, still in my hand, a shade of blue that could make you weep, that brilliant; the lettering describing what was offered and the image of the hotel, dull gray-black. I pored over the façade. One floor up, there, behind the curtains, we had stayed, right above the entrance. Why was I hanging on to this? The words touting what it hadn't been, *Your Oasis in the Heart of Amsterdam.* I wasn't dragging this along to New York, I had plenty else to tote around. A relief is what it would be. I shifted it to my other hand, held it there for a while. Perhaps I should memorize the address—if ever I felt I needed to go back and ask, "Please, for room number 3—do you need a key to get out?" I gripped it, with both hands ready to tear. I hesitated. Wasn't as easy as I thought, I couldn't do it, rip up where we had been, even if our night there hadn't worked out. With great care, I put the brochure back in my bag.

How much longer before that limousine came, black no doubt, like a hearse, perhaps the same driver as when I was picked up for my father's funeral, black coat, black cap. "There's enough time, Missus," he had said then, but the second we got to the house, the procession began to move toward the cemetery. I had had enough of my stepsister's gifts, that ride in the little airplane, no bigger than a double bed, when had that been? In between what scares? Enjoy the view, she and her husband said, of what was being done to prevent another flood from causing destruction in Zeeland, as had happened more than a decade before. As soon as we were over the estuaries it began, the picture-taking, "Ow, Jim, your elbow, you're hurting me, the corner of your camera is digging, let's swap seats, this is ridiculous, Jim." I couldn't move, I sat pinned against the window. What was he seeing, in those barriers that were supposed to stem a flood, that he couldn't hear me? More looks, other looks, a pilot-can-we-approach-the-dam-from-a-different-angle look. We rose away, hurtled closer, the camera pushing on whatever part of me was nearest. It took the pilot to say, "Your wife has had enough." Only then did he hear. He probably never even saw the roll of film developed, it could still be in some camera shop in New York. Or lying around somewhere, tossed onto something.

Why was the radio still blaring behind me, Belfast, Vietnam, would it never change? I bolted into the kitchen, turned it off, something gained at least since I was a kid and my father was king of the set, relaying whatever war news there was.

I stormed into my stepmother's bedroom. "Taxi," I forced out. My God, she was dusting her dresser, what a thing to be doing today. "It's late," I protested. "You're just like your father," she said, reaching for her inhaler in case of wheezing or worse, another asthma attack. "He had no patience either, the first one to get up, the first one in the doorway, 'Come, Magda, hurry,' hurry to where? Had it been to a reception at least I could have understood. He was like that to the very end, a man in a hurry to nowhere. The car will come, when

Nel organizes something you can relax." I wanted to put my face against hers, bury it in her neck, nuzzle up like a baby searching for a nipple. I stepped away, afraid of my hunger. Where were my children? I wasn't going to turn into my mother, who, after our Jopie died, forgot there was still life around her.

Into the living room, fast ... I checked through the window. Yes, where they should be, under the eaves, protected from the wind and dressed in everything right, up to and including their rain hats. They were poking around the border of pebbles with a stick—looking for fossils? They'd found one the week before, when Jim was here. In that same piece of garden he had talked to them about sex, how it was done, right there, near the clump of ornamental grass and the rose beds, red even after all this rain and wind, a setting as pretty as a picture postcard. I kept taking it in, so someday I could say, That's where he sat with you, bare arms, bare legs, it was summer, a warm one in Holland that year. It was around four in the afternoon, I'd add, the sun was at an angle, the time when roses give off the deepest smell, having absorbed the day's warmth. Your heads were close together, bent.

I wondered what words he had used, which, traditionally, perhaps should have come from me. Like their first bath, he just seemed to know how. And the middle-of-the-night bottles, he took care of them as well. It didn't matter if he'd be tired the next day, he said, it made him feel at rest, holding our babies.

Next I stared hard at the velvety green of my stepmother's chairs and couch. The armrests were very nice to touch. If you rubbed a hand across them one way, the color intensified, and it paled again if you reversed the motion. I took in whatever I could, obsessively, the tiny silver objects, cheese cart, wheelbarrow, windmill, and lighthouse, all left where Kathy and Julie had been playing with them, on the glass table. I forced in other possessions: the wooden sewing kit with legs of its own, the package of cigarettes Magda would offer to a delivery man, "Take one." Anything to shut out this morning, last week, even further back than that.

Jim had wanted another child; he'd talked about it all year, this spring, as recently as my birthday, the same birthday when we discussed writing the book that was going to retrace my childhood. "No more," I said, "we already have two kids, that's plenty, I'm not starting with diapers all over again." Three, my teeth chattered, as in his family, he being the last one, with a rescue mission for which even a gladiator would have been unfit. Had he expected the same of our third child? If one more could have helped ...

Over the pots of sansevierias that decorated my stepmother's windowsill, I smiled at my children's backs, *lieverdjes*, Mommie's *snoetjes*. Shouldn't I be talking to them about their father? I couldn't just ignore that they'd never see him again. Shouldn't I ask them how they felt? What, I tried to think, had Sini said after Mother died? After Jopie's death, what had I been told? "You need to be kept here," but it was Miss Pul who'd said that and made me stay after the other kindergarteners had left. When I finally got home, did my mother do or say something?

If anyone was ever going to hurt my children—of course you hurt them, Jim, couldn't you have predicted that?—I'd kill. Like Johan would have done for me.

During the war I prayed every night, without making sounds. Thank you, I'd say to no god in particular, thank you for everything. And I'd ask for everything, that no bomb would hit, no soldier would come and take us, that we'd all wake up again, Rachel and Father too, in their war beds. Even on days when I hadn't felt like spelling it all out, I did something, the thank-you and please parts. I'd gotten out of that habit too, dropped it on the day of liberation. My lips began to move again just as they used to, even shaping the same words, still stuck in the creases: bed, bomb. What was it called again that got announced this morning? When the phone rang, and what was the word I was going to use that would make it all better. Heartack? I might never be able to say it without looking away.

From over to the right, past where my children were still scratching around for a token of early life, came the clopping of wooden shoes. Old Maria, a neighbor, her nose to the ground, leather shoes wrapped in newspaper under her arm for later, once inside the church. How many masses had that woman attended in her life? At two a day? What did she have to confess, own up to, whatever? I seemed to be hearing music, but none was playing, a requiem as I had heard in concert halls in New York and sometimes sang with my choir. No more for me, now I surely could not sing anymore. As it was, my voice used to drop out whenever those around me swelled and I'd have to wait till the lump in my throat sank and the notes stopped blurring. When we finally got to perform and Jim and the kids would come, I'd look up as often as I dared to where I knew they sat, to assure myself that my new world was still intact. Six hands I'd see, waving.

Over to the left, on the piece of road I could see, the house we had moved to about one year into the war jumped out, when we had still been a family, though without Jopie. Police came to it one Sabbath. Jewish men shouldn't be working that day, and with the synagogue no longer open, they'd be at home, an ideal day to check on who was still available for roundup. "We'd like to speak to your father, little girl, where is he?" Still in bed, I answered, "shall I call him?" "No, they said, it's all right." He wasn't home at all, he'd had been gone for weeks. Where to, that time?

It was close to eleven when we left Winterswijk. No one talked, not the driver nor my stepmother sitting next to him. There was only the sound of windshield wipers swishing back and forth, lifting sheets of water up. Visibility was poor, made more so by sprays of water whooshed by the back tires of whatever car was in front of us, weather like the very first time I met Jim, a winter rain then, we went for a walk anyway, his umbrella covering both of us, and he offered me his arm, which made everything just the right size, that new city of Boston and the Charles River where, drops clattering down on our cloth roof, he recited a verse by Edward Lear, not the same Lear as in *King*, I asked, "The Jumblies" it was called, creatures, heads green, hands blue, who went to sea in a sieve, "You'll drown, everyone cried, The sky is dark and the voyage long."

How do you tell children that life is one continuous good-bye, that with each day the end comes a little nearer, each step, each touch, each sound, whether you're around to hear it or not, cars tooting, trains whistling, boats hooting; how do you explain that people you're close to, or thought you were, can just vanish?

My body tensed forward, my children's hands in mine, I searched for markers that would say how much farther it was to Schiphol Airport. When we were almost there, a plane deafening overhead (please not mine), my kids asked, "Is Appie okay?" My God, where could the cat be? "I'm sure

Daddy took good care of him," I said. "I'll call you, and by the end of the week I'll be back to pick you up." They nodded. "We know," they said. How could they trust me? Their father had said the same, "I'll pick you up."

Before the car drove off—the driver would be careful, right?—I saw that they had their arms around each other.

Part III

THROUGH A CLEARING in the mist a building showed, panes of glass and some lettering, AMSTERD RPORT. With even more imagination, you could picture the word SCHIPHOL too.

"Annie." Sini said, from her window seat. "Do planes take off in wind?"

I shrugged my shoulders. How did I know, how did I know anything? What was light could be dark ... I touched my forehead, ice on ice. Maybe I was dead too, just hadn't been notified yet.

"If the weather gets worse, I mean. All right, you don't have to answer, I know it's been a terrible morning, we won't dwell on it, not good for you. But what if the motor isn't screwed in tight or a wing drops off. Did I tell you that Rachel paid for half of my ticket? Wasn't that nice of her?"

Teeth clenched, I nodded. Rachel ... somebody else to whom I had to tell the truth—someday.

"I wish I remembered what I put into the suitcase, my makeup of course, I don't even take out the garbage without putting it on, but for the rest, who can be sure with the little warning I was given ..."

Looking past her, I watched a truck drive towards the plane, then watched it disappear.

* * *

When the wind blew a little more and sharpened the view I saw what I took to be wagons, faces peering from openings across the sides. Some are recognizable, look, there's the aunt with the drip at the end of her nose and the smell of garlic on her breath; and my uncle Mozes but no potato, maybe he has one in his pocket. Where is my cousin Hannie's doll? Real porcelain, it could say Ma-ma when bent forward, she never went anywhere without it. And my grandmother is there; I'm allowed to comb her hair with my fingers, this way, that way, I rake, a penny she'll give me for it, three of which buy ice cream, vanilla between wafers, if the weather was warm and the cart appeared in the marketplace alongside the tree heavy with proclamations I'm just old enough to read, the MUSTS and MAYNOTS. Her hair needs combing again, strands are covering her cheek like a sheet masking a corpse. She's beckoning me, her hand, stretching. I make no move, I sit and watch the windows slide away. You cannot hear them leave, no whistle shrills and no grinding of wheels thunders over. Does the grayness outside, that mist, stifle everything? As they were led away did they ask themselves, "Why did we always worry so?" And fight, about what again that made us not talk to each other for years. Did they think at all? Had any of them been turned in by one of my cousins, very beautiful, nose as delicate as on a Christian's face who, after she got caught, made a deal with the enemy: If you let me go, I'll bring you others, I'm taking you to safety, I'll say, and they'll trust, I'm a Jew like them ...

* * *

I kept scanning Sini's window but no more faces showed out there, only arms, up, pleading as in the sculpture commemorating the bombing of Rotterdam, a figure, heart torn out, the statue I saw from the railing of the ship when I first left for America and kept seeing as the strip of water widened, those hands reaching high, trying to push back the sky where my stepmother's voice could still be heard over the shrieking of gulls, "Don't forget, cotton gets boiled, flannel not quite, and if a man over there were to look at you, have an open mind, anyone Jewish is fine."

Jewish ... I was going to make something good out of my stay in the States, however long or short it was going to be, something of my own making, and Jewish was not part of it. I wouldn't mention the word "war" if, during my nine days of crossing, I did get pressed about a past—why should I? Nothing showed, no number on my arm, no scar. No ducking when strangers approached but if someone insisted I'd dismiss it fast. I'm only interested in "new" now I'd say, busily trying out other lines as well, more suited for starting afresh. Your language has many words, some playing a trick. Worsted has to do with yarn? Are you sure wash days are dog days? And who could guess that lazy Susans do so much work ... To think that my *English Book* at school had dared

call itself *Complete*! I could've been walking around making
a fool of myself. *Flaky dryness, oily shine, externally caused
pimples* ... Amazing how much practice it takes to have a
conversation other than where you were born, Winterswijk,
don't bother to pronounce it. Why did you leave your town
and country? Something else I might be asked. I needed adventure, I'd beam at whoever wanted to know, not bothering
to remember it had been my father's idea after my stepmother thought of it first. *Catsup, nifty, snafu*, why is wrestling
pronounced minus *w* minus *t*? Don't have those letters then.
Same with *thistle* and *whistle* there too you shouldn't say
everything. I did have a real conversation already, with a
lady who had heard I was from Holland, from my cabinmate
probably to whom I said: "Had a good sleep?" every morning
and "You seasick too?" This lady wanted to discuss a certain
boy with me, Hans Brinker, she once read a book about him.
"Hans Brinker?" I had to be honest, "Of him I never heard."
He stuck a finger in the dike? To ward off a flood? "See you
later," I said to her as she had to me. I wanted to specify how
much later. Not necessary apparently, or perhaps not done
with an American, so I too walk on, back to the pile of magazines in the Reading Room, the special place on the boat
where you could forget you were alone, surrounded by water
and that the clock would say again, sixty minutes gained, or
lost. Sometimes I just sat there holding a magazine on my
lap and I'd stroke a page, so shiny and smooth, like brushing
a finger across piano keys, and notes would spring up into a
new-old piece of music that swayed and rocked, you could
almost picture arms forming a cradle, you in it; and I'd have
to remind myself I was there to add to my stock of words.
Easiest Ever! Naturally Lovely!

* * *

Nothing new about the plane, we were still being held. From her window seat, Sini kept filling my silence. Could this morning's announcement flung from the phone have been a mistake, a faulty diagnosis made by someone ignorant? Maybe it had been a heart attack. People get those, here one minute, gone the next, very tragic, especially for those left behind. Life will go on. *Sizzl-licious, Photo-perfect, Stir-N-Drop ... Heartack*, yes, that would be today's word, already coming along nicely, no problem for someone who crammed in and memorized Foreignland-language before, *mouse/mice* but not *house/hice* and who when other babies were still in the gurgling stage, not only addressed the woman who cleaned house by name, Aadje, but also noticed something special about her. Six toes she had on one foot, I once saw the extra one when she changed into slippers, eleven toes that's what it must've come to altogether. I'll tell your boyfriend, I threatened, later of course, stringing word after word takes time, I'm going to tell him, Aadje, I say grandly, one leg already raised, unless you let me ride on your back, as she crawled around with a rag, ridding floors of prints made by other people's feet. Whoosh the little calf away, I low, lustily, as the Yankee Doodle song learned at some Americanization course where Werner in his native tongue rhapsodized about his mother's liver dumplings and Françoise bemoaned the fact "there was no bread here who looks good." Faster, Aadje, I roar, we can't stay on this patch of floor forever. "Annie will go far," the pediatrician said and Father repeated to anyone with or without ears. Faster yet, I demand, pulling the straps of her apron, pretending she's a pony with a slightly off hoof sliding backward and forward on hands and knees. No, don't trot to the station, that's where trains lurk deep inside shadows.

From the chaos spinning inside my head a train breaks loose, the one Jim and I were on last week or the week before that, after the nightmare in Amsterdam, whenever that had been, who can be precise? People, feet, wheels, all run into each other, until I can no longer say what is totally real, partly imagined, or how much I finally allow myself to see. It was an ordinary train, definitely, you needed tickets to get on and buying them we were asked, "Roundtrip?" "One way," we said, "will be fine, to Amersfoort."

Our compartment was warm, stuffy, it was hard to breathe. Jim was dozing, his chin on the unbuttoned part of his shirt, his book *Islandia*, about a young American in an imaginary country, lying in his lap. I stood up, turned the window down until it went no further—why hadn't I done that sooner?—and stuck my head out. I began to feel freer, perkier, looking at new wallpaper will do that, Sini would say, gives you a boost. Across the rail, glistening in a ray of leftover sun, two people were lazily pedaling their bikes off into the dusk—going where?—they seemed in no hurry to arrive. In a meadow a farmer, raking up sprigs a machine had overlooked. A milking stool, turned over. Shriveled grass, then ditches low on water, but no heron nor a cow in sight. And no sheep, not even one flipped over onto its back trying to get cooled off, a position you wouldn't wish for it, of course, they're never able to scramble back up. "It's too Goddamned hot for 'm, Annie," Johan's voice, loud and raucous, I would have liked to hear but only the train blustered, cutting through a landscape marked by drought.

I leaned out farther still. There had to be something familiar. A chicken coop, door open, but nothing inside; squares of silent meadow, a carriage wheel flung onto a heap of gravel, a sandy path that meandered on for a while. No sign yet of a house, no activity behind a window, no one idling near the roadbed. A wave, anyone's in response to mine, would have reassured me that not everything had withered, that our two days away and the night in the hotel had been different all right, but not alarming, not overly so. That lamp, though, bent at an angle—the way De Gaulle walked, I had mocked—jutting from his hand like a spear, as if he was about to attack or to defend himself against someone; me. If only I had put my arms around him or made light of it. "We're a funny couple, Jim, one thinking love and about to strip, the other one on alert like a soldier. Is this a new way to have sex?" We could've laughed, perhaps. We didn't talk about it afterward, not in bed where we finally inched back to trying not to disturb or notice each other. Neither did it crop up at breakfast, in the special room, ceiling so low I was convinced he'd want to leave. He was fine, sat, chatted, ate. He did not look right, that was a real worry, he was more tired now than at the beginning of his vacation, everything wore him out. "Go see a doctor," I'd tell him, "as soon as you get back, Jim, Doctor Blitzman, couldn't be easier, right in our building." On his way to work he'd all but trip over the man's office, same doctor he went to with the kidney stones and the mysterious hives that went away. Was everything that was happening this summer caused by the book I hoped to write? The prodding up of memories, who knows how that affects the ones you're close to ... I would discuss that with him too, when all was calm again.

I never heard him stand up or walk over to the window. He was asleep, I thought, I had just turned around to check. Before his hands landed on my shoulders, I felt his presence

right behind me. As unobtrusively as possible, I pulled my
head back in, I even wondered what shoes he wore, peculiar
as that seems.

Someone else must have entered our compartment, I
thought, when a body began to close in on mine, someone
sinister, intending harm. How could I have said, Jim, is it
you, by any chance? My own husband, who had never done
anything unsavory before, who couldn't have been sweeter
all these years, eleven, not quite, who expressed his love all
the time, in Russian too, and so very well in Dutch ...

One of those trucks coming to a halt? With papers listing
who'll be taken away next? I peer out Sini's window. Fog I
see, traveling toward her and me, *sshht*, or army boots will
scud over, black, tall as chimneys, I saw them in Winterswijk. I was alone, not quite home yet. One pair first I hear
come down, I quickly cross the street, where I still hear
them clack. Hide, we need to hide; I know, Father, no other
word of yours ever sank in deeper or stayed around longer,
it never left, it's with me first thing in the morning till my
last thought at night. At the table he'd deliver it with each
meal, the rag Mother wears against her headaches firmly in
place as the runner embroidered by her hands protects the
piano from his battle cry, Hide-hide, his fork jabbing the air
to point up our predicament.

Turn your head away, Sini, I wanted to urge. Still voice-
less, I touched her elbow, to warn. Don't look at what's men-
acing through your window, something old has come back
from a great distance in time, something we had long put to
rest is thrusting forward and all mixed up, arm-foot-belly-
leg and gone again, faster than a thumb riffling the pages of
a flipbook, before tumbling back to ordinary Plexiglas like
airplanes are fitted with, scratched up and wet, no cracks

like in our summer room, three in the window I counted, I counted them aplenty and beyond, door welded shut. What just welled up and flowed off again, a piece of door? From my apartment yet, metal with its own see-through area, I saw it explode one night, just before I came to Holland, this summer, my suitcase already packed. It woke me, had Jim seen it too? A ball of fire larger than the sun lifted that door off its hinges, you could just step out to the terrace or be inviting danger in, but when morning came and I cautiously opened an eye it was still standing there, un-nicked ... there was something calming about its intactness, it made you believe nothing had happened, at least nothing that couldn't be ignored.

My name, coming from dangerously close. I all but jumped out of my seat. That Sini, rattling me like this. I should've been given a fair warning. Look at 'r, all rigged up in a suit, of frightening color, aqua, wool at that. Hadn't she ever paid attention when I told her how hot New York got in August? Either by letter I did, Jim always adding a note, or with my own mouth when we got to see each other. Should I have screamed it from the rooftops?

"What a busy morning," she was saying. I nodded again. "Had I only known about this delay, Annie, I wouldn't have hurried so. How did I get it all done? Take my arm to the doctor for some kind of injection, smallpox, I think, ow, I feel it, run after a visa, do laundry, pack. I had no idea what to bring, other than my beauty case and a nightgown, I only packed wool now, I remember, I hope that's all right. Looking at your face I can see I was wrong, but I've never made a trip this far, and at such short notice, to New York yet ..." And what would she get to see once we got there? Apartment, funeral parlor, morgue. Briefly I put my head on her shoulder.

When she began to stroke my face I sat up again, as far away from her as I could get. I wasn't going to be softened up and start the sobbing. Not until I was good and ready. At some private time maybe. Maybe never. A person has the right, no, duty, to turn into a rock. To be sensible.

Why does my neighbor across the aisle keep rustling his paper, it was making me edgy, all that folding and unfolding, FLOOD IN CHINA, TRAIN WRECK in a place I could not read but from which people also would not return. And when he wasn't doing that, crinkling disasters, he did the other, asking anyone in sight. Will this plane ever leave? As though it mattered when we'd arrive. Too late, whatever time clocks might say.

Out of the corner of an eye I watched Sini chew her pinky, just as she used to during the war—I had timed it, how often? Until it was red and sore. Still she wouldn't stop, couldn't whenever she was upset and didn't want me to know. What had it been? Other than what did come out, turning old, no one will ever look at me again, I might just as well be buried for real. Why did she say that? I'd think when she'd slip out of the room. She'll be back, won't she? Is she near a window? Should I go get her? Or did no sound at all mean she was still all right?

I checked the plane window again, everything looked the same, misted over, strings of drizzle navigating their way down. In the country, roads would be soggy by now, squishing at the slightest pressure of feet, tree trunks would have darkened, leaves would look different too, some turned under; even spider webs would have altered shape, slack with the weight of drops.

I remembered something said decades ago but as fresh as if I were hearing it right now, "You'll turn into a murderer yet," my stepmother's prediction after I flung the paring knife through the kitchen, during another one of her lectures on peeling potatoes the right way. "Skins shouldn't snap when bent between fingers," lifting a chunk of peel to demonstrate to my ears I had done it wrong again. The knife didn't even graze her. Still ...

I shouldn't make Sini wait any longer for what I had to say, it wasn't right. When we ascended maybe, or during the drone of landing, which would muffle it some too, make it not sound quite as raw, quite as naked, surely before we got to my door I'd force out the more accurate word regarding Jim's death, more precise; more like it. If she didn't already know. "Can't fool me," she always said, "I know you as well as though I made you myself." Once over the shock, if shock it was, she'd crush me in her arms, before boarding she had already tried, and I'd backed away. "My child" she'd call me again. I wasn't her child, I was no one's child, I was on my own.

I still had Jim's voice though: "Why not have a sound-track made," Rachel had suggested, "so Sini and I can at least hear you get married." Only Jim's "yes" was on the re-cord; I couldn't talk then either, overcome by what the rabbi had just wished: "May they frequently be together with their loved ones." How so? I thought, if I can't even see my sisters on my wedding day. We'll visit them, Jim promised, soon. With what? There was the Harvard loan and the money he sent his mother each month, hardly as much as his sister and brother sent, but still their father earned. But help from him, who had left her for another woman, she refused. If I saved whatever I could from my job, a clerk at Parke Da-vis, even though Jim said, "You don't need to work," and if there were no children right away ... Going back, if only for a quick look, couldn't be put off, Rachel and Sini might be gone—dead was too scary a word, leaving me, the youngest by quite a few years, still around. How could I walk through their towns and point, That's where they lived, I believe that's where it was, perhaps new trees were planted or they added a room that I have trouble recognizing where I am, a tourist in my own land.

In America, I fought being married in a synagogue. I still answered "none" when asked "what religion," or "Jewish, sort of" if I felt I wouldn't be harmed by my answer. No, no memories. In a synagogue, no matter how far away from the temple I started out in, I might still see myself sitting between my mother and grandmother, who's loosening her bonnet. "Make me beautiful," she says, bending her head so my fingers can reach.

"Let's keep it easy, Jim, no fuss, no bother. Can't we go to City Hall, get married there? See a Broadway show afterward, *The Music Man*'s supposed to be cheery, nice story too, a swindler can't read a note, deceives everyone but it ends happily and very moral, you'll like it. He even ends up with the librarian, what could be better?" "Getting married in a library," he suggested. Books might calm his mother, who had a problem with separations, and for the first time in years she'd be seeing Bob again, plus his second wife he insisted on bringing along. "And no dressing up," Jim said about himself, "Bermudas will be fine." Imagine, in January, in the state of New York. In the end the synagogue was done for my father and stepmother, they'd be traveling from far and would expect tradition.

It was cold the day of the wedding but no nip, perfect skating weather, Jim beamed as when he, and his brother and sister would glide along the canal in front of the stone house at Lock No. 12, Idy waiting inside with cups of hot chocolate. The snow-packed roads opened something in me too, it made cars, chains around wheels, emit tank sounds or the sounds made by ramshackle bikes without rubber tires underneath people who shook up and down. At least they were free, Sini used to say at that other time in our lives when we sat together.

A few stars were out, I looked up as soon as I stepped from my friend Betty's car, which had gnashed to a halt in front of the synagogue, separated from Higgins Funeral Parlor, Inc., by a hedge made even taller that night by heaps of snow frozen into spikes, a formidable barrier to where I was about to become a wife, six encounters after Betty introduced us the winter before. Another star showed and the possibility of one more. Sometimes in Usselo when it was like this, winter and dark, I was allowed out, down the stairs, into the kitchen, out of that door too, over to the side of the outhouse where, Johan standing guard nearby, I stood and hugged the wall for a while, not breathing deeply. It would make you cry before you could stop it, to be given this gift, of almost-normalcy, and it occurred to me that perhaps there was something of a shepherd and heaven, not only on Opoe's Sunday-school picture pinned up in the room but away from there as well.

To think I was a bride just about, in a dress from a fancy shop yet, Betty's idea. "My stepmother would approve," I told her, looking around. "You didn't even have to rummage through the racks, they gave us chairs and brought what they thought was right for me." Ecru, the saleslady said, walking over with something else I wrinkled my nose at before I even got a good look. At least it had no ruffles, nothing puffy about the sleeves, the skirt not so wide you could turn it into a set of curtains. "A most becoming color, isn't it?" the lady said to Betty. Finally I saw it that way too, after envisioning it as the color of wheat ready for reaping. Too bad it was the wrong month for tulips, I would have liked to carry something that had flourished in the soil I grew up in. The wedding bouquet was of chrysanthemums instead, flowers of the end of a season.

The synagogue door opened again. I needed to go in this time too, instead of standing there, staring into the cold as though I had no place to go, like the matchstick girl peering at someone else's feast. A big step, marriage ... if you thought about it too long you'd say "No." It wasn't like testing bath water with only a pinky or the very end of an elbow, all of you would have to go in. Perhaps I had been too impetuous after all, too much in a hurry, even a week sooner I had suggested, on Jim's birthday, "I'll be your present." But he wanted our occasion to be a celebration of its own.

Holding the lace hanky borrowed from when Betty was a debutante and her gloves from the same occasion, I kept looking up. Hopefully I'd be an all right wife when it was time for the special nightgown Betty said I needed, a see-through—right to where a man shouldn't, my grandmother would warn, "he might give you a bellyful of bones that would stick out and show the world what you had done, behaved like a gypsy," whose music I loved, made you want to sing along and move around on your chair, *Komm mit nach Varaszdin, so lange noch die Rosen blühn.* Where was Varaszdin they wanted you to come to at the time when roses were still in bloom? And hopefully, after the honeymoon, four days in the Poconos, and nights of course, I wouldn't be too upset I'd be moving, deeper into America. I had come for only one year ... "See you then," my father whispered behind my stepmother's back, when we said good-bye. At the end of the dock. The boat still moored.

I moved a tiny bit closer to where I was going to wed. I

might be living in America for ever now; be buried here too, near some highway, cars whizzing by. What a thought! But if you lived somewhere else long enough, far beyond the three and a half years I had been away, what would stick in your mind of where you were born—other than war and who was no longer there? Everyday things, would I remember those? Already I no longer knew how much a centimeter was, an inch had no meaning yet, let alone feet, yards and whatnots. Miles. My trunk was already on the road, the HOBOKEN USA label gone, Detroit put in its stead, wedding presents stashed on top of the possessions I had come with, shoe polish, a can opener, two sets of washcloths, good ones for the top, cheap ones for the bottom, the mezuzah from my house of birth, the poetry album with rhymes by Hannie, Carla, and my mother who started hers "TO MY DARLING ANNIE." And the photograph of the Oosterveld house given to me by Johan so I'd never forget that part of my life.

Clutching someone's arm that trembles, like mine, I walk into the synagogue, onto the runner, faded red, over to the wedding platform. Halfway there, Jim and his parents stop and come over to get me. Jim's eyes are laughing, his mouth dances. I let go of my father's arm and take his. The pianist, who doesn't know how to play but charged little, grows tired of trying and gives up. The rabbi begins to chant the prayers. A blessing then. And the question, first asked of Jim: "Do you take?" And then: "Do you?" I had heard it all right but my voice could not find a way out then; any more than now.

Slowly I opened my eyes to the sound of the man folding and unfolding the paper. On my other side, Sini, still chewing her pinky. Through her window rain showed, a curtain of rain no umbrella could keep at bay. I verified it anew, yes, rain and a lot of it, anyone out there would get drenched.

Where were my kids? On what stretch of road? Back in Winterswijk already? Where they wouldn't cross streets, would they, alone? Get their hair close to the stove, get sick, have a bad dream they couldn't tell to anyone but each other? Or were they still only halfway to Winterswijk, sitting in Rachel's kitchen, where at least English was understood. They would've gotten there safely, that driver was good, nothing to worry about with him, they could be in front of something steaming right now, soup, ha-ha, beautiful soo-oop. When life went back to normal—for a second I focused my eyes on the ceiling of the plane, my lips twisted in almost-prayer—when my kids would be home at least, I'd make going to bed special for them. No lullaby, neither Jim's asking for peace nor the Dutch one about sheep walking outside, another myth, there were no sheep when you needed them, I looked, leaning as far outside that moving train as I dared. I tried to bury the fear of Jim's hands, but east, we were going east, he and I, like those other trains that never came back. It was around suppertime and hot still, I am sure of that too. The sun was sinking, red, bleeding into blue, about to blot into each other, a few leftover rays were still puttering around the rails in some sort of game, come hither, go yonder. I see them come up, glistening razor-sharp or I'm falling, I cannot tell, it must've been a case of madness on my part, or an attack of nerves such as I had never had before. Your time has come, those tracks shriek in voices of pure steel, You cannot be exempt forever! The machine-gun fire, rat-a-tat, that violence inside the walls of my mouth was back too, castanet-loud, *sshht*, heed the kids.

I'd read to them at night, they loved the Alice book, soo-oop of the eeeeeevening, a word Jim would draw out until you were sure there was not enough breath for one more *e*.

Go on, Daddy, they'd giggle from their beds. When finally he ended the *es* with *vning*, I could hear them laugh from the kitchen where I stood inside my apron depicting an indigenous scene, tulips on a bed of yellow. No, not the Alice book, it could pull you down a hole you couldn't scramble out of. A different book, Kath, Jule, shall we? Where not every word would have Jim's voice pulsing underneath mine. How about the Pooh one, you'll love it or love it again, fine too, a bear of great reason, a frisking-around bear, a humming-to-himself bear and you know what about, a honey song, of course.

I nodded a few more times, toward Sini, who was going over her morning again, the visitor's visa she had to get, trip to the doctor, all the phone calls she had to make, whom she said what to and who answered whichever way, her boss in anger, "This is clearance week, Sini, I had counted on you to sell whatever underwear hasn't moved." And on. And more. With embellishments. What if it had been Sunday still, wouldn't the consulate have been closed? And what if Charles hadn't been around to drive her first to the doctor, then to Rotterdam for the visa? "Did you feel we were moving, Annie? No? It must've been the wind. If it's this scary already, still at the gate ... I've never flown before ... No storm, I hope, although I'm happy to say, strange word to be using today, forgive, it must be the state I'm in, which I shouldn't of course be saying either, not to you, but I did see an emergency exit, I always look for one in a hotel too, I need to be able to flee ... Fires scare me, Annie. Why, come to think of it, I don't know. I've never been in one. Johan used to talk about fires a lot, remember? Well, he did, and always in connection with a storm. 'Spreads the flames everywhere until there's nothing left, not one Goddamned plank ...' What's the matter with me, talking such nonsense, come ..."

I shift another hairsbreadth over to the right, away from those arms I'd never want to get out of, once in. On the boat at least, no one had been on my back, doting. She was lucky I didn't snap at her. Vigorously, I begin to tap a foot. Where to? I could enjoy myself, *sh-boom, sh-boom*. Into the Entertainment Room, of course, I went there once, after leaving the Reading Room and the magazines for the nightly quiz I gave myself: *Are you in the know? Measurably more, measurably better, long wear, less care*, and after another look at the ship's clock for how early still or how late already. "Join us, folks, don't be bashful. You by the door," I was contemplating whether to go to bed or what, "Yes, you also, come on in for a go at the Lindy, it's popular where we're going." Hophop, me too, and although my feet have never been the dancing kind before, they navigate across the floor with the same ease as the ballerina from *Life* magazine offering a vinyl tile, *Cleans quicker! Yadadadadadada*, over to the land where ice cream is considered a food, eat up, people say, It's good for you! *Boom-bah-do* and where more than one family *bah-do-badoo* has a television set so the rest of the town doesn't have to trample around your window trying to catch a glimpse. Goodbye to my old national anthem, the "Wilhelmus," funereally sad, hello to the new one already heard halfway across, very appealing, they played it, *O say can you see by the dawn's early light*, two lights yet, not all the way red and not totally yellow, a figure then rising from the water, I saw it from the deck, Statueoflibbedy, Ennie, that's how my cabinmate—shoes with fruitclips that came off, pear, melon—pronounced my name, Welcometoamericahopeyoulllikeidere. It must be Jesus rising from the water, I thought, with all those prickles around the head? Or else my stepmother dominating my arrival as she had my leaving.

The rings of the telephone came back, incessantly like a refrain you want to shake but can't. I try, my tapping intensifies, upupup, barely coming down as longlong ago, around the Feast of Saint Nicholas, him I do not fear, his helper Black Pete scares, face blackened with shoe polish to make him resemble a Moor. Upup wentgo my feet, fast, into my pajamas, Zwarte Piet might be lurking underneath the bed, aiming for an ankle and carry me off to Spain in his burlap bag. He would, everyone says, if you hadn't been good in the course of the year. Or when a lie crossed up your forehead.

A stab of pain bolted in. I shut my eyes against it, tight. Could this condition of Jim's ... his mother hadn't been totally ... either ... Could that, that strangeness, get passed on, like the color of eyes or the thickness of hair? A gene? Wasn't there a law, someone's name on it, Mendel, first name? Last name? Sweetpea Mendel, yes, a wonderful smell, before your nose got to them you always knew, around here must be where they grow, white, pink, and what could pass for blue or lilac or purple, all beautiful. Who cares what Mendel thought up and got printed in some book? Nothing to do with us. Only the good you got from your father, we won't bother with the rest, those few odds and ends that didn't show till the last couple of weeks. And turned for the worst sometime during the night between Saturday and Sunday—a day he used to like.

My God ... don't flatter Yourself, mentioning Your name means nothing, Rachel still calls on Mother whenever a car skids by as her husband still yells for his mother long gone but, my God, the cat must have been a witness, a herald waiting by the door. Get away from my legs, Appie, I can't have you rubbing up against me, that's bringing it too close, like being touched by death itself. And stop your meowing, the where and exactly how you keep to yourself.

* * *

From the plane, aground still, my eyes crept to a portion of
my living room, to the piece of furniture Jim once assembled
for books and records, one of them loudly proclaiming his
"yes" the day we married. I push that piece of wall away and
scurry on to the picture of three horses, each one prancing
off in a different direction, and the other print dating back
to Jim's bachelor days, of a tiger posing ferociously, Chinese
lettering perpendicular to a leg, urging it to do what? Pull
that one up, too, and bolt? To the spot then on the opposite
wall, where the new print was going to go and perhaps already hung, the van Gogh we'd bought in Amsterdam, where
we'd cut loose from everyone. "It'll be just the two of us,
Ann," as we had set out together. "Let's buy this one," we
both said. It was of a farmer, like Johan, back of his pants
patched, scythe held ready.

I forced my eyes back to the length of wall where his
"Yes" rested in the fold of a microgroove and where shelves
held his books—big ones on art, smaller ones on poetry, and
a dark blue book that could help you get out of a hole. All
right, a dictionary. You can't go around accusing people of
something horrendous simply on hearsay, can you? Mouths
can be wrong, especially when it comes to words, words
have to be checked—some other time. On to books equally worthy of attention; on democracy; abolition of slavery;
the beauty of the poor, of peasants, of anyone downtrodden
for whatever reason; books he and his mother talked about
when she came to visit, clothes hanging off to a side, lovely
sketches for the children under an arm, Plato on her lips, or
Jean-Jacques Rousseau, whom she could quote in French,
probably backwards if necessary. Talktalktalk, all weekend

long, "We need to go by the books, James." As she had done when her children were born, hugging Jim when an author in vogue recommended. "Those books on your shelves tell us what life ought to be like, James, perfect for everyone." He'd agree, voice calm. "I'm shocked, James, at how that came out—it sounded as though it no longer matters to you, which I've been noticing lately. You used to be even more adamant than I about the world and how to view it. What happened?" "I've become a realist, thanks to Ann, I'm a husband, a father, someone who goes to work in the world you still see as perfect. It isn't, it never will be, the people in it have faults, they don't act the way you want them to, that's a mirage you need to stop clinging to or you might end up with another breakdown." Her eyes flashed underneath eyebrows angling up, "If I relinquish what my mother stood for, James, if I stopped believing in paradise on earth, I'd be disloyal to her. What that woman didn't do for her ideology." (In an agitated whisper, as if a spy could listen in), "She joined the revolution, became an ardent socialist, forbidden party, czar was a beast, she said, 'I'll do anything' ... underground activities ... risked deportation ... Siberia. And you tell me to be a turncoat? That would be a disgrace, I'd rather suffer."

Long after Jim joined me in bed, where I had gone to study recipes—nothing fattening, no legumes or anything else that could turn into sugar, and nothing chewy for the other difficulty the five-year stay in the institution had given her, no more teeth of her own—long after Jim had come to bed, she still tore around the apartment, she couldn't settle down, it seemed, to get some sleep. "Why doesn't she at least lie down on the couch, after we turned it into a bed for her, Jim?" "In a minute she will, Ann," but he was listening for her as well. In the kitchen now, making herself another cup of tea? In the bathroom then, I hear her flush and turn on the faucet, washing her underwear, no doubt, which she'd drape across the shower bar, from where it would greet me first thing in the morning. There, by our door again. Would she barge in? Needing to say more that couldn't wait ...

My thinking eyes swerved back toward Jim's dictionary, next to something on sculpture and *The Hours of Catherine of Cleves*, my gift for his last birthday, surprising him because it wasn't a sweater or the cufflinks I had been hinting at. I could barely restrain myself not to give it away, "It starts with a *B*, Jim, not bread, not building, second letter an *O*, that's all I say—and that it's decorated, but I won't tell you with what." I had gone to a museum to buy it, a miniature painting on each page, colors so vivid they leaped at you. He hadn't even gotten out of bed before I gave it to him, unwrapped, so he could see it immediately. "Do you like it, Jim?" He did, and he was touched I had given something that really mattered to him, a book on art.

That dictionary I mentioned—only to myself, of course, no point in babbling about it out loud—you should see the cover, blue and very dignified, as though you shouldn't be bothering it with a foolish question. And the size ... it could barely be lifted, that complete, it even had *Oxford* in the title, much higher you couldn't get. Of course, it has an *S* section, what a question, *stumbling block*, *sugar beet*, *suggestive*, *sui generis* ... You couldn't find more esses anywhere. I wouldn't have to check all of them, I could do what Sini and I used to do, close our eyes and, each armed with a pin, prick a word on a page and guess, or make up what we'd like it to mean.

Don't think that after the war I had no experience with dictionaries; in America I walked around with one that fit in the palm of my hand so right away I could look up what dumbfounded me: *jumbo melons, luscious and ripe*, a triple giggle. During my coffee break I did that, at the Grand Union in Pearl River where I got a job, all on my own, after carefully studying what to say: "Might you here have a position that could be filled by me?" I think it was the manager I said that to. "I am four days ago from Holland come." "Cheese country," he said, and into the basement I went, over to the slicing machine in the dairy department. Swiss Domestic (57 cents a pound), Loaf American (Pasteurized), Cheddar (aged over 60 days) as yellow as the weekly pay envelope, "3519" written on it, no decimal point, no comma. It was a pity I opened it. And took stock.

That rain, still flogging the airplane window, darkening whatever light managed to seep in, bloodlight, of a day as it comes up, and chickens, having found their way out of the coop, start treading behind the rooster for their first morning walk; when in my apartment the alarm goes off and Jim, after having shined his shoes over and over, starts his exercises. It's important, he says, it makes for a better day. He does them with the same intensity as when he ran from tree to tree on our way to Usselo for the visit to the Oostervelds and he needed to bolster himself.

Each morning he drills: jumping jacks, scissor jumps, eagle jumps, his feet bare on the strip of floor between the dining and living rooms, along the shelves weighed down by his books and the record player sent by his sister when she and her husband went to the Caribbean to live on a boat. Eleven minutes a day he spends working toward his goal, level twenty-two in the booklet issued by the Royal Canadian Air Force. He doesn't find it easy, he's no athlete like

Phil, the All-American boy to whom girls used to flock the way books took to Jim, whose arms are out and up, like the war sculpture in Rotterdam that reaches toward the sky for solace that the earth cannot supply. His back is lit by the ceiling lamp bought with money sent by the enemy turned friendly again, the amount determined according to guidelines on pages 4, 6, 7, 9, and 15 of Booklet A. Were you arrested, robbed of freedom? In camp? Jail? Did your children die, your parent(s), your husband? Jim filled out the form and sent it in, "Don't be silly, Ann, why not take what they'll give?" "One guilder for each day of hiding?" I said, angry at the value put on my sitting it out: "What about nights? Don't they qualify?"

Thudthud, he goes, with each exercise, which gets repeated until it can be properly done and in the prescribed time. He's getting close, he says, to the level the chart recommends for his age, by fall he might get to it, as early as September perhaps, the month in which he rereads *The Hobbit* and gets started reading *Islandia* again, a story akin perhaps to what Jim and his friend Pat sketched, map and all, of their made-up world. Someday he'll turn it into a book, he says, "You realize I could write, Ann, and be good at it too, if only I set my mind to it." It's Tahiti he escapes to on evenings when he laments that in spite of all the hours he's slaved away at the office he still hasn't made enough progress and the deadline seems farther out of reach than before. "I'm getting out, I've had it, I'm off to Tahiti, for a life underneath palm trees where the skies are tinted by fire, don't think I'm not cut out for bumming around a beach," and I, terrified he'd quit and go to another broken company, offered what would keep him where he was: "Tell your boss to give you help or let him wait. They won't fire you, you're the most dedicated worker they've ever had ..."

Tahiti ... had Gauguin gone to live there by himself? Got the urge to flee? Left his wife? Left his children? Some louse, that Gauguin, they would've formed a fine pair, he and the deserter I was married to, they could've been sitting side by side swapping tales of what used to be. I could look up Gauguin's life, if I wanted to, in an art book Jim brought home from Idy's apartment, where she died. Of a presumably natural cause, after having shut herself away again from anyone at her front door who insisted on getting in, fictitious or not.

What if I had killed myself and left you like that, with two small children, yes, it's you I'm talking to, Jim. Gauguin is dead and cannot hear. What would you have thought of me? You would have just accepted it? No questions asked? "Ann must've had her reasons, or believed in a cause so deeply that sacrificing her life was worth it." Like those protestors against the Vietnam War who did away with themselves. "They did it for the cause, Ann." "How," I said, "can an act of destruction solve what it supposedly is against?" "Sometimes you need to do something drastic, it shakes people up, makes them aware, of the horrors of war in this case." "What about their wives?" I said, "or their children who counted on them, or parents they might still have, brothers, sisters, you name it?" "If by immolating yourself you could be saving many lives, it's worth it, don't you think?" "No," I protested, "each life stands for something, ask anyone for whom the mere act of breathing was punishable by death."

What made you do it, Jim? You were the one who always said, "You have to stay rational in life, there's no need to mash potatoes with a sledgehammer." What was so bad that you could not go on? What were you thinking? Or were you not thinking at all? No, I'm not done yet, there's lots more dust to be raised. "I love you so much I could kill for you,"

you said more than once. Was I supposed to have known you meant yourself? Shouldn't this, of all things, have been discussed? Would have been a lot fairer than doing all of the dishes or half of the cleaning; after all, I'm the one who has to carry on, whether I want to or not.

You'll be fine, Ann, you're a survivor, I can almost hear you say it. Which doesn't mean I have no feelings. Or the right to an opinion, accent and all. Was death more irresistible than me? Say something, Jim, come on, don't step away as on the night I told you to work for a healthy firm, to stop trying to resurrect, that's a word for the Bible, an afterward word, invented so death doesn't seem so final.

Sitting within walking distance of the terminal still, I see my street, three thousand miles away, in Manhattan's 13th Precinct, where the brother of the deceased cannot give the police any history, or any reason. A pleasant street, lined with trees, one, the ginkgo rescued by Jim some snowy winters ago, gracefully reaching up above the windowsill behind which, on the living-room ledge, my copper and pewter sit, reminiscent of the farm, the measuring cups, pots, and ladles, all wedding presents from my childhood country, and the bronze giraffe I once bought for myself, its legs as long as its neck.

I watch the walls grow dim, you can barely tell what decorates them or make out the spines of Jim's books, those that gave rise to disputes with his mother, whom he called Idy until we married and I urged him, "Call her Mother so I can say that too"; and the adventure books he couldn't wait to get to again. Only one title still sticks out, the words *I Ching* printed in grass-green lettering, *The Book of Faraway Knowledge and Wisdom and Change*, yours for the asking when contemplating a shift in life. Then the shutter of darkness closes over that book, too, before surging on toward the ledge where it sweeps over my pastoral ornaments, and the giraffe stowed in my trunk the first time I ever crossed the ocean, pretending I had no past. In my bedroom, eleven hours after the time for which it had been set, the alarm still cracked; sounding like a human cry.

Tarom-tarom, I don't know on what day or at what time, but I'm on my way to say good-bye to my brother, he's in the hospital a few rooms away from where my mother would die, in a corner of Winterswijk I cannot find but where I walked all right. Down go my sticks, up comes the sound, from the drum tied to my belly, I'll make it louder, I want Jopie to know I'm coming, he's departing soon, why or for how long my sisters don't say, but far away they imply, where he'll never have to see a cow again.

Louder yet, I need to drown out the train that thunders past, only not past, I'm still on it, standing by the wide-open window, Jim behind me, his hands on my shoulders. Together we faced the outside, the bits of empty meadow sinking along with the sun, and dust swirling up from the roadbed. I felt his chin now too, on top of my head. We did not talk. Often we stood close and not a word got said; I liked that and I'd lean into him, getting closer yet. This time only my eyes moved, to the left, where we were going. But no house yet, no spire of church or a water tower promising that our station was near, only more dusk was streaming in. I roused myself to say something. "It can't be much longer, Jim, trains in Holland are reliable, there has to be something very unusual for there to be a delay." No reaction came. Below, the steel clicking of the wheels kept coming up as the scenery rolled on, empty, no rain and too much heat, this summer in which streets teemed with people up till all hours, dancing and clapping and shouting anti-America lines into the stillness of mourners back from Normandy, where the Allies had landed when life had not been worth living. To Arromanches they had gone to pay respects, to Point du Hoc and other cemeteries filled with stars of David and rows of crosses like so many addition signs, another one and another one, and those marked UNKNOWN.

No, I never heard Jim getting up in the train, his eyes had been closed last time I looked, napping, I thought, *Islandia* in his lap. I never heard it fall, it might have made it less startling when his hands came down on my shoulders.

The eerie thoughts were back, about strangers contemplating doing harm ... I had not written one sentence yet of the book that would show something of the past and already everything spooked me. As in Scheveningen, on the beach, long before the train ride.

It had almost seemed too late for a walk but it was warm still, no breeze, and the kids were asleep. "Go," Sini urged, "enjoy yourselves." Arms entwined, we left, stopping only to kiss, on past the area of cafés, until the only light, the red and green dots coming from the stone jetty, were behind us too. Shoes tied around our necks, we edged on, stopping more frequently and for longer. No one else seemed to be out on this stretch along the North Sea, which must be pulling and drawing whether you saw it or not. Would we make love, I wondered, here, on this bed of sand? Jim would be happy to, "I've come home," he'd say when he entered me, whether at home within eyeshot of the mirror or wanting to on the porch of his father's house, where in their bedroom, Bob and his new wife were having an impassioned discussion on art. Only our voices could be heard the evening of our walk on the beach, Jim's wanting to stay, mine urging him to leave,

"Come, Sini must be waiting, Jim." He didn't have to know I had to get out of all that darkness broken by nothing.

Our train clanged on. Jim's arms moved up, to the top of the window frame, and dropped again, back to my shoulders. I rolled the window halfway back up, waiting just enough so it wouldn't seem a show of panic. Imagine if he knew what thought had just shot through me: that I might be shoved out, like the postcard an aunt and uncle forced through a chink in the siding of their train, "Mail please if you find." Or were we supposed to jump off together? Lovers at the end of their rope. His body began to press mine. I pushed back. He yielded, immediately. I chided myself ... danger sensed didn't mean it was there. His body returned, exerting more pressure than before. I sat down, out of breath as though I had been fighting for my life, something I still can't be sure of, even today. Had he, in an unpleasant way, been trying to convey, *Something scares me, Ann*, only I can't say. In my mind's eye I saw again the Delft tile that he had bought for his secretary, of a little guy pushing a wheelbarrow many times his size.

I picked up *Islandia*, a book about a dreamed-up land, a young American's adventures there, which Jim normally didn't open till September. "I thought I'd get an early start," he had said, and, "How come, Ann, that a book I love so much I keep rereading it, you won't even consider?" I put it next to me on the seat and waited for the train ride to end.

Jim stayed where he was, hands on the casing, gazing out. Is that how he traveled through France as a student, swearing he'd return someday? "Next time I join you in Holland I will, Ann, without you if you won't come." His head was tilted now, one ear up. What was he listening for? A train coming in, perhaps? He had hoped for that, waiting in the leaky boat alongside the stony house, and from the window-sill in the apartment afterward, a train that would bring his father to release him of his burden. He didn't blame Bob for divorcing Idy, he once said, she was a trial to live with, without saying what that meant. Neither did he say—did he even know?—that far from where he grew up, he had begun to break down. Nor did I recognize until months later that I, in a different way from his mother, had not been easy either.

The plane began to move. The terminal disappeared from sight. We went around a bend, onto a runway. The humming increased. Sini took my hand or I hers. The roaring became louder. A baby cried, another one joined. I listened, not to that, but for someone to unsay what had been announced twice at the break of day, first by Phil, voice clipped, then by Vinny's call, a neighbor. When he and Carole finally returned from a weekend away their phone was ringing, it had all day, Ruth and Sam, they were worried, Jim had never shown up for his day in the country at Lake Celeste. It wasn't like him to miss a train, they said, then not to let them know why. He wasn't on the next one, either, nor on the one after that. No explanation, and no one in my apartment was picking up the phone. "If you have Jim and Ann's key," they said to Vinny, "you must let yourself in, take a look."

I shut my eyes to bring in something lighter. The boat? That had taken me to the brand-new land, trunk at my side? Not the farewell part, that I didn't care to see again, my father's back as he rushed into his car, nor Sini's hand that wouldn't stop waving from the quay, something airily light was needed, that dancefloor *yadadadadadada*, where I hopped to the Lindy and kept hopping even after my stockings had slid way down to my ankles. But all that came through was a place I could not picture, where an ambulance must have taken him to "afterward," his body obscured underneath a sheet or inside the bleakness of a bag, that unknown site where they keep you until the next of kin comes in and says, Yes, it's him.

Part IV

IT WAS EVENING when we got to New York; hot, humid. My hands tightly wrapped around the bag containing Jim's letters, I walked off the plane. "Was there another woman?" Sini had dared ask just before we landed. Another woman ... "All that man ever did was work and come home, Sini." Late though. Very late, at times. Who? Phyllis? Cleft lip and bad skin, why kill himself over her? He helped her with statistics, that was all. And his secretary was old enough to be his mother. "Don't you want someone younger?" she had asked him at the interview, "As you can see on the application, I am fifty-six."

"What does it matter?" he'd said, "You're here to work, that's it." Another woman ... Just like Sini to come up with something that outrageous, like her other theory: murdered in his sleep. "New York is a dangerous place, it's all over Dutch newspapers, Tourists Beware, they say, especially at night. Why do you live there, anyway?"

Vinny and Carole had come to meet us; and Lloyd and Dottie were also there, friends made during the school strike, with whom Jim had had dinner on his last night alive. "It's been a busy day," he said when he entered their apartment. "I shepherded an English potter friend of my sister's around, he wanted to get a feel of the city in between flights. We went all over, downtown, Staten Island Ferry, Chinatown, uptown. We kept on walking, the UN, Pan Am Building, then over to the West Side, to the top of my office building." He had worked there the night before until one A.M., to get his credit-reject study in fine shape. And he took Appie to the vet, something seemed wrong with his eyes. An infection, he was told, easy to cure. "A tube of salve was lying on the counter," Carole said, "not hard to find at all; right away I put some in, I think it's helping, Ann."

We crammed into Lloyd's car then, all six of us. Vinny turned on the motor. "Take me to where Jim is," I demanded. "I want him to know I came as soon as I could." "Morgues aren't open at night," Vinny said. "We'll go first thing in the morning."

But when morning finally came, too much had to be done. Papers to be signed. Trip to the bank, before the account got closed and there'd be no money for a while. Obit, important too. Died at his home. "How?" I asked. Just how. No details were offered.

The going was slow, the roads leading away from JFK were crowded, buses, vans, taxis trying to merge. "Was it an accident, Vinny?" still clutching at what could've been, "An intruder, maybe? Did he do it on impulse, perhaps?" While sleepwalking? On our honeymoon he did, and again in Detroit, first night in our apartment; must be checking the window I thought, making sure no snow can creep in.

"No accident," Vinny said. "Not on impulse, and no intruder, everything was in perfect order. He knew exactly what he was doing, the police said, to have succeeded so well the first time around. His timing was perfect too, after you and the kids had your vacation but before you returned and could've walked in."

I wanted to touch Vinny's shoulder, say something, "I feel bad not only for myself, for you too, who had to find him." I could neither say it nor touch him, any more than thank Sini for having come with me.

Was there a note? I wanted to ask but couldn't. Jim wouldn't have left without leaving one, precise as he was, always hanging up his coat on the same hanger, same spot in the closet. There might not have been an opportunity to mail an explanation, aerograms gone, no more stamps in the house, no time for the post office. There had to be a line or two lying on the table or stuck in the typewriter, where he knew I'd look. A couple of words that would make going on easier: "Got a tumor," or something else he thought beyond a cure. As soon as I got into my building, I'd ring Dr. Blitzman's bell, whether he had office hours or not. "What did you tell my husband this time?"

He probably never went, it wasn't like him to ask for help. I imagine myself away from Sini and the car full of friends, who are no longer talking.

I'm back in Detroit, a Sunday, the weather perfect for a ride. The car wouldn't start, that VW that was forever giving us trouble. This time is it something easy, Jim, that you can repair yourself? So it wouldn't cost. All morning he fussed, "In a minute I'll give up, Ann," all afternoon he tried, when it got to be dark and the flashlight shone on even more parts that refused to go back in, he was still saying, "I can fix it," even after the car was towed away he was convinced. That was a car, though, not his life ...

My face showing nothing, I stared across vehicles blurring along, Jim's letters pressed against my stomach, force-feeding into me lines five and one and eighteen, "Love you most of all in the world"; that hurt as much as anything else.

To say something so precious, then trample on it? How often had he thought, *That's the place, this will be the method*, then postponing it, the weather not right, the season wrong, too many clouds, not enough rain, until finally something told him that turning back would be worse than going through?

My mind leaps to part of my bedroom, the telephone, next to the gray metal box, the piece of paper with the numbers where I could be reached while in Holland, pasted firmly inside the lid—Jim's idea, so with one glance he'd know what to dial. He wouldn't even have had to get up from the mattress, had he wanted to hear my voice. What if his note, which I was getting closer to and closer, said the opposite of love—I couldn't even think of the word right now. Only as far as Schiphol I offered to take him, not much of a sacrifice, barely an inconvenience. No wonder he said no. And I never called after he got back home, afraid I might hear something that would interfere with compiling more questions for Johan, such as "Did you like having Sini and me around?" hoping he'd say, "Especially you, Annie."

"Note?" trembled out before I realized. Again Vinny shook his head. "And no doctor's appointment had been made. Checked on that too."

"Autopsy?" I asked of Phil when he called, the day after my arrival. I know he wasn't sick. Still ... might be important, for me, for the kids. But he, having been the one to peek into Compartment 16 at the morgue, said his brother had gone through enough. Leaving him alone would be the kindest thing to do.

Through the open car window a warm breeze fluttered in, thickening the smell of gasoline. Sini kept wiping the sweat off her face. Carole just sat, not a hair out of place. Once in a while Dottie or Lloyd mentioned something, their voices equally flat. "Can't figure it out ... been racking our brains ever since Vinny called ... a joke, we thought ... even laughed ... he was looking forward to getting you and the kids back, Ann ... That, he said at least twice ... we don't understand, he seemed fine." More came out later, intermittently and in snippets that I memorized and connected.

"You should've seen him eat when he came to see us, right, Lloyd? Not a morsel was left on his plate, striped bass with crabmeat filling." And he praised the special bottle of wine they had bought, lifting his glass to the chandelier to admire the color. "We wanted to make the evening a celebration, welcome him back. He loved his time in Holland and finally meeting Rachel and you, Sini"—who couldn't wait for all that English to stop—"'She's just as Ann described her,' he said, 'warm and beautiful.' Ooh, and that you're planning to write a book. He was so proud of that. 'I am married to a woman who writes.'"

He told Dottie and Lloyd about the polder we had gone to, the piece of land that used to be Zuider Zee, Jim driving my stepmother's car, she in the backseat with the kids, I ready with the map opened to the route Jim had traced out and translated into miles, seventy about, to the edge of the polder, a trip they'd be interested in, knowing how they liked to travel outside the tourist stops. "This one surely was," he said, the land had been there for ages, submerged, then delivered from all that water. "An awesome achievement," he called it, awesome, a day he would not easily forget, the land so pristine it had barely been touched, no plow had yet broken up the soil, nothing had been built on it yet, a wide-open landscape. Walking around it, he told them, gave you hope that you too could be transformed, that the possibilities you had only dreamed about till then could still be reached. A most reviving experience. "Reviving," Lloyd repeated, "that was exactly the word he used, right, Dottie?"

"I did not see that," I said; "I only saw that he constantly needed to nap that day." Every few kilometers deeper into the polder he'd had to lie down again, along another ditch lined by trees no thicker than a wrist, where the kids ran after a cat they spotted, black and white like Appie, happy there was something they recognized. And again, he put his head in my lap and slept. My stepmother and I worried we'd never get back to Winterswijk before dark.

It was almost midnight when Jim left Lloyd's and Dottie's apartment. Who had ended the evening? They couldn't remember now whether it had been Lloyd or Dottie who had jumped up. Definitely not Jim. "Maybe I'll stop off at the Sroges," he said, "considering how close I am; I haven't seen them for a while."

"At this hour?" Dottie asked. Jim looked at his watch. "You're right," he agreed, "I'll be lucky if I get in six hours of sleep, I have to catch an early train, I'm spending tomorrow with Sam and Ruth, in the country. Yes, much looking forward to it."

Before he headed to the elevator and out to the street, Dottie offered him their car for when he'd go to the airport to get the children and me a few days hence. "I might take you up on that," he said. "Might?" Lloyd said, "Don't be silly, take it."

"Okay," he answered, "I'll call you when I need it." "That

we were the last people to see him, Ann, we had no idea." Should they have paid more attention earlier that summer, they agonized, when he joined them for an afternoon at the beach and in the middle of a conversation he stopped, looking intensely sad. "It's because he misses his family," we thought, "and how nice that he'll soon go over to be with them."

When we passed the cemetery along the Long Island Expressway, that endless stretch of tombstones abandoned to the din of cars, somebody mentioned the funeral.

"You need to make arrangements, Ann." I nodded. Of course—that's what you do for dead people. What kind of funeral, though; we'd never discussed dying. Old age, yes, this spring, when it came up at a party, one friend guessing it would be like this, another one like that, and I, "As long as the coffee still smells good, the potatoes melt in your mouth and the sun streams in through your window, I don't think it'll be so bad." "It doesn't work that way," Jim said, sounding as though he knew exactly what he was talking about, as if he had reached old age already and was thinking of his life's end. I didn't ask, neither then nor on the way home, and it was still on my mind, as weeks later I preferred not to know what was underneath his "Watch it or I'll lose control," after letting me argue—"What's the use of more life insurance, we have trouble with the premiums as it is, you said. If there's any extra money, why not invest it for now?" and he wouldn't fight, wouldn't answer back; until that warning "Watch it." Like a rider at the end of a lease you do not bother to read, convinced it has no relevance.

I tried to count how many other times he had all but said "I won't be around much longer." When he was working with Pat on their imaginary world where thirteen months made up a year, that one called Month of Storms, and announced, "Time is running out." Had that been a warning, dressed up as a story? "We need to dam up the river or all will be lost ..."

Barely able to breathe, I realized that on top of everything, I might also be poor, whatever policy did lie around wasn't going to pay out, considering what he did. I had to find work that brought in more than ten dollars here, twenty there, thirty-five with luck from translations done at home and by teaching Dutch at an agency. I needed a regular job like other people, study shorthand again, work on my typing. I'd do it, there were mouths to be fed, kids', cat's, the landlord's mouth too, the rent due in a couple of days and with the new lease coming up, higher no doubt. "Stop obsessing about work," Sini had said on the plane. "First things first." If I could only remember what that was ...

A horn blared, another one crescendoed in answer. Perplexed, I glanced around. Why were friends taking me home? Was Jim at the office still? What about Sini, though, what was she doing here? I lifted my glasses and rubbed my eyes, stinging from what had come back in again, my last glimpse of Jim, his back, as he hurried into the KLM bus, me just standing there, waving from the sidewalk. "Did you love him?" Sini asked, earlier, while still on the plane. "I thought so," I answered, but what does loving mean when you hold back when it counts? "Of course, I had no idea he was going to kill himself, Sini, please, what kind of question is that?" But that something was very wrong, I knew, and I didn't want to be around to see. "Doesn't that make me an accomplice at least? I should've gone home with him, no matter how scared I was. At least it would've shown that I cared, Sini." "A de Leeuw," she said, "does whatever it takes to survive."

And the thought had come back about her and Johan doing something in the stable. If, that is. I suddenly felt such pity for her, remembering her ruminating out loud: "I'm turning uglier by the day, who'll ever want me?" It would've been all right, Sini, if Johan made you feel desirable, if only for twenty minutes. She never brought the stable up with me, her little sister whom she had taken on as her child. For that she would've needed a friend she didn't have.

It was easy to be so understanding now, nothing bad had happened, but what if Dientje had seen, if, of course, something had been going on? Would I have been thrown out too? Or would I have followed Sini of my own free will? And might that have been the only time I loved enough to have bolted after someone without thinking what would happen to me? Or not even then? All those questions, all those intuitions, locked up and set aside.

And along with Sini I had looked off toward the airplane window where the shade had been drawn, in color and size an old calendar page, discarded ages ago, I thought. But stockpiled; like so much else.

Death cries suddenly. Hear it? There, again, I jump way holding my stick, that magic noisemaker I need to defend myself. *Tarom-tarom*, I go, trying to muffle what's coming from the burlap bag Father has deposited in our backyard where it waits for the rabbi. Not with his pencil, that he uses for picking his ears when teaching Hebrew, not with his bare hands either, those, I've overheard, are for grabbing underneath the skirts of his big girl students, a reward for being the best, the others are supposed to keep their heads down on the Book of Moses, the slaughter for our Friday soup gets done with his knife, blade razor-sharp. He runs his nail across it to make sure that, according to ritual, only one stroke will be needed to do the slashing.

Whose vocal cords are shrieking at the loss of all that red? Is it coming from a neighboring coop? Or from my own throat, as big drops splash around the yard where they turn into eyes that keep looking up until they disappear into soil, chickenmuddark.

Or are those screams coming from Jopie's bed next to my small-sized one? Something is wrong in his belly, he might have to go to the hospital, where I too was taken, but why? The chickenpox were gone. "It's for your safety," Mother explains, in case another bomb pushes us into the night air again, the worst, she says, for someone still on the mend. Not so. Waiting for her to come and see me, that is the worst.

The car keeps pushing on, toward somewhere; home, they say. Home. This winter past when Jim and I were making love he yelled out, as he came, "Mother." If I had asked him afterward, "Did I hear right?" might he have acknowledged? Maybe even explained? If I had wanted to know.

Afterward, still cuddling Jim, who was already asleep, I wondered whether we both had been hiding all those years, he only inches away from the picture he grew up with, a Japanese-looking boatman out in a storm. He took this seascape from his mother's apartment after her death.

Jim hung the picture I saw as somber near his side of the bed. One night, this past winter too, he wanted to change places with me. "C'mon Ann," I remember, "I've been sleeping against the wall long enough." "Why complain about it now, Jim, you never minded before, my one leg has to stick out of the bed." I tried, a few seconds, I couldn't do it, I had to be able to get out of bed fast. "In case of what, Ann?" And I had no answer.

Mother ... isn't that what children cry out, and men on the battlefield, when they're afraid, or in pain? He had to have seen her fall apart, he lived with her, taking care as though he were the adult. More than once she went to an institution, to get better. The last time, for the long stay, an aunt committed her but blamed Jim for having walked his mother, who he thought of as a free spirit, through the gate.

Had I known what I wasn't told until much later, that right after his mother's death, Jim, at a debate on lessons from the Holocaust at his old Quaker school—where at the end of each year when everyone's grades got posted, Jim's score always the highest, and the student body, sixty or so of them, would marvel, "He's bound to rise to the top"—had I known what he had blurted out at that debate, that Hitler may have been right, that Jews are inferior, would I then have understood? That he was accusing himself?

You were a good son, Jim, you were not responsible for her death. You did not cause it, nor what she was like before.

He never talked about his mother's death; I did not ask. He would not have liked me to, it was not done in his family. I'm not sure how much I sensed, but what would have stopped me from probing, as much as anything else, was the terror of encountering a depth of pain no drum would have been loud enough to still.

Shortly after he started his last job, which offered a real future, he mentioned the word "psychiatrist." "Not that it's helping Idy," he said, no longer calling her "Mother" by then. "Still, I ought to see one and talk about her now that she's living by herself again, I have some names in my office, some lunch hour I'll go."

"Do you have to, Jim? What if they got wind of it at work, couldn't that hurt your chances? What d'you expect to find out?" Jim had Idy's eyebrows, wide, and eyes that flashed when a comment was not received well or a question annoyed him. Nothing else, right? He wouldn't be needing help himself, would he? He was more thick-skinned, he always said, not as sensitive ...

Through the part of window that showed between Carole's and Vinny's heads, the evening looked limp. A thought struggled in, circled around, then struck. Where was Sini? My God, gone too? There she was, sitting right next to me, my one hand resting inside hers, the key to my apartment enclosed in both of ours.

The nerve, I used to think that my marriage was better than hers, better than Rachel's and my parents'. None of their squabbling and whining, I promised myself minutes before Jim and I stood on the *bimah* smiling, where, the rabbi said, that very morning he had read the portion of the Torah that talks about the exodus from Egypt, to be celebrated in your house.

We used to, at the seder, *baruch atoh adonai*, Father says, fast; he's afraid the food will get cold, worse than any plague, he says, Blessed are thou, *elohenu melech ha-olam*. He gathers more steam, turning several pages now at once. "Ies," my mother complains, hands pressed against her headache rag to stop the pain from moving down, "Is there nothing you can do in peace?" and he, in response, telling her to shut her mouth or else. On a family outing when he says that, he begins the "or else" part by steering the car toward the nearest tree, to show her he means it. Why? I am allowed to ask at the Passover table, in a language I do not understand, Why, *halailoh hazeh,* is this night different from all other nights? Already peering toward the window that overlooks our backyard where the prophet may appear, Elijah who, Jopie knows, that for sure, will free us from all hurt.

Next week, after Sini was three thousand miles away again and easily that many hours, at night, except for the breathing coming from my kids' room, the footsteps of the neighbors above, and the off-pitch scales, sung out by the woman on the other side of my bedroom wall, there'd be nothing. The rattling of the air conditioner. Wind across the terrace. But no one coming home, no matter how late, to crawl up against, no face to bend over, stroke, or put mine next to. No one to talk with about the day that lay behind or the ones still to come.

What if Jim were right and I'd get to be eighty years old? Wished, he said anyway, at that party last spring, "I'm sure of it, Ann." More than half my life might still be ahead? More than forty calendars, how many days would that make? And evenings and nights in which to review and reflect where else I had been at fault. I was no better than my mother, "We can't go to America, Ies, what'll become of our meadows?" Refusing to see the enemy was already at our door.

A storm of anger rushed back up. By your own hand ... even the timing was perfect, with me away, the kids gone, "All that fresh air will be good for them, we ... you ..." you said, getting confused about who had mentioned what to whom, whether it was relevant or even added up. "The fare is the same whether we stayed away for three weeks or more, which would be good for the book too." Years ago when you played along the Delaware River, dark you said, and beautiful, the fog at times so thick you had to grope for a trunk of poplar or a branch of sycamore to make sure your feet would stay on the footpath. When you and your little friends—I'm getting to it—played those war games, whose side were you on? *Actor, pretender.* I couldn't stop, lips closed, heart pounding, I roared on: Schemer, Block-Island-next-year-sit-on-the-beach-in-the-sun-rent-bikes ... Liar.

This anger was choking me. I'd have to get rid of it. Next I'd be doubled over in bitterness. I thought of Johan. "That's not what I saved you for, Annie." I know exactly when he said it, after two springs had already stopped off, still one more to come, that April, when I stepped out on the road, hanging on to his hand, I had trouble walking, legs might crumple or fold. "The war has done something to you, Annie," he said, "I see that now, but don't you go into the world with hate, nothing good comes from that. It'll get better, already you're waddling a little easier, eh?" Sometimes I forget, Johan, about not hating, and I slip up.

I wasn't going to waste whatever time I had left spewing, some prospect that would be for the kids. Already I'd made one mistake: when Julie had asked "Who'll take care of us now?" and I'd said "Kathy and I will." Sure, I took it back, Jim. "Mommy will, don't worry!" But who knows what will remain with Kath?

I may never be able to talk about you with them, Jim; I don't mean cause of death, I'll get that out. But what age? Twelve? Eighteen? For which one, oldest or youngest? Rather in remembering this or that good time, or the fun we had, we did have some at least, no? Or was your laughter not real? Did it substitute for something else, the way I transformed clouds that went by what I claimed to be my window "then," especially in winter when clouds were easy to spot, no linden-green yet and no walnut leaves blocking the view, and each morning, from as close to the glass as seemed safe, I peeked, what kind of day was it going to be? Any traveling to be done? A face I could accompany? Look, the beginning of a hill showed that I could climb across or slide down on, whatever I wanted, and there, was that a flowerbed appearing in the frame? Yes, white petals, white stems I could pick. Perfect for dressing up. And to drive out the madness inside.

Ultimately, Jim, what will I remember? Already you seem a shadow. What did you sound like? *Look* like? A round face, yes, a tuft of hair before the strip of baldness, I'm sure of that too, rough hairs growing out of the mole on your hand, something else that doesn't easily slip one's mind but when I shut my eyes and try to force all of you back, you either appear to be a very gray person, not a face I recognize, old, prophetic, or I see another figure, beautiful, pure, dressed completely in white, shoes, jacket, pants, tie; and I run, no, not to you, away from what I see ...

More expressway, other drivers intent on making the best possible time. Remember, Jim, the first dinner I ever cooked as a married woman? Sweet-and-sour sauce over tongue? Ended up on the ceiling, you on a ladder, night after night scraping off all that sugar and vinegar? Of course you know, I didn't have a double-boiler, I improvised one, easy enough, two pans jammed one into the another, it blew up, sauce on my face, in my eyes. I was lucky you walked in just after it happened. We went to the hospital, remember?

Downtown Detroit, the same hospital Kathy was born in, where Jim brought a book of sonnets to read to me during contractions, kisses on the breast, dewy morn, the breeze is at the door again, I was the one who had packed the *Wall Street Journal* that I planned on scanning for whether national retail sales were up or down, could be important for our future, three Reisses in it, just about. I might even read about a job, get him away from the department store he wouldn't leave, where he wouldn't ask for a raise either, not ethical, he said, they're doing poorly. Like the chain of clothing stores his boss went to next and got Jim, whom he thought of as a son, to work for him again, another bubble that burst.

Those hives he came home with when he started at his final place of work, the company with a future, where they gave you a raise on each anniversary of being hired. Like a celebration was how I saw it.

He never complained about the work, though—the amount, yes, but not the nature. The way he talked about it you'd swear he had wanted this all along, cash surrenders and term life. Must've felt like lifelong ... and how come only now I saw that those dead-end jobs he used to have, those short-lived illusions, might actually have suited him? He could still tell himself they were only transitions until the time came for something more unusual, something more important. What if he had announced, I'd like to go back to school, study law, late as it is. What'll I tell the A&P? my voice would've said, after my face already had. That my husband has a dream?

Even if someday he would have become chief financial officer only I would have beamed, he wouldn't have cared, been embarrassed would have been more like it, a defector from himself. He had wanted to be part of a cause, something on the order of civil rights, or work for the Tennessee Valley Authority, government-ordered power to be sold at cost. He said something like that the first time we met, in Boston, Betty took me there. "Bring Annie up next time you visit," her Ed said, "I have a friend I'd like her to meet."

The idea of an MBA came from the army, where—because of extreme flat feet, he used to laugh—he was assigned to an accounting unit. He set up a control system, installed it, ran it. "Why not prepare yourself for a business career?" a superior said when he left to go on his Fulbright and study political science. "You'd be a natural, Specialist Reiss." It had taken some digesting, he had never considered business before, it was all but looked down on in his family, "money-grubbing," they called it.

While in France, beholden to no one for a change, Idy still in good hands, he began to rethink his future. Labor law? He did have a slot and a full scholarship waiting at Yale ... Become a journalist? One in the family was enough, Bob, who happened to be an excellent one. Start a newspaper? Bob did that once, *The Penny Press*, which had netted not even that.

Getting an MBA might not be a bad idea, take out a loan, part-time work, summer job, GI bill, he could swing it. He had enjoyed that army job, been good at it too. A sure bet, that's what he kept hearing, Colonel Prunty's voice, whether he was sitting in a café or on the train admiring the scenery that went by. "You're a natural, Reiss. You can't go wrong with that kind of confidence ..."

With my free hand I wiped my eyes again. If Sini could hear my thoughts she'd tell me, Cut it out. Be sensible and move on—as we said right after the war. If I don't go back to a time when we both had hope and do it now, all that may stay is today and the day of the phone call—had that been only yesterday?

On a Saturday we met, Jim and I, in the state with more consonants than teeth in a toddler's mouth, MaSSaCHu-SeTTs. "I've loved the learning part," he said, about his em-bee-ay. "All I need now is to figure out how to put it to use." By that time we were at the Mapparium, the building in Boston with a globe you could walk into and see the world on glass panels, illuminated, Holland too, although Jim had to point it out to me as he showed where his grandparents were from, Vitebsk and Bialystok, book publishers on his mother's side. On his father's he wasn't sure, Bob never talked about them.

"In my case it's all cows, Jim, either walking around or no more; we had butchers too." When he laughed, the creases in his cheeks were deep enough to put a finger in and stroke. What was the matter with me, we had met, what— three hours ago? Betty had warned me, "Don't be forward-hasty, that's for secretaries on the make." Such a sweet face, though, how could she have said "not attractive"? He was better looking even than Rossano Brazzi, what movie had he been in again? I just saw it ... very romantic, about love, yes, three girls, three coins, a fountain and who'd be blessed ...

That Betty, what she hadn't done to help me "make it" in America. Talked her employers, Lederle Laboratories, into hiring me. With only two fingers I typed the names of difficult diseases, glaucoma, elephantiasis, hydrocephaly— "waterhead" in Dutch—onto index cards. She found me a tiny room in the same house she lived in, next to her suite, where she not only improved my English but also, martini in hand, held forth what it meant to be the best possible American "in these nineteen-fifties, Annie," a long list, big-bucks-big-house-big-car, like her Chevy, say no to Communism, nice-house-fine-china and now this, someone to marry, potentially, "and not just any old student, no, from a hallowed school," Bettie said, "Ivy League." He was a genius or her Ed "would have nothing to do with him." I had never known a genius, let alone been delivered to one to whom I had to talk. Good. Not yet. He was beginning a geography lesson ...

"In many parts of the world, Ann, there exists an imbalance of opportunity, here, for example," his hands sweeping between the Indian Ocean and the South Pacific, "or there," his entire body bent toward yet another part of the globe, "and unless something gets done, the gap between the industrialized nations and the underdeveloped countries will keep on widening ..." So lucky I had lost all that weight, probably one-fifth of me was gone, not to forget where else I looked new and improved: legs shaved, armpit hair no more, hair on my head one big curl. "Is she the same person," my family would ask, "we waved good-bye to?" From near the herring cart, "Have one, have two, can't find those on the other side." The shape of her nose, perhaps, that's still the same and the color of her eyes, otherwise, no. It's me, all right, I'd say, the way we like to look, sophisticated. "We," as though I already belonged ...

I should be adding to the conversation, another one of Betty's tips, Engage in the topic at hand...

"... in today's world, yes, Jim, it is not enough to be concerned solely with oneself, no, cultivating your own garden, sure, without reference to the needs of others, of course, I feel to be more than a little immoral, I agree." I had never sounded so good, all that glass around us made for great acoustics. "Besides, that attitude is inexpedient." Beautiful, I offered, hoping it fit, flattered he thought me up to his words and didn't take me for the newcomer whose vocabulary stretched only so far.

I measured him with my eyes. If we stood a different way, facing each other, say, and close enough so our clothes touched, would the top of my head reach up to his chin? In my new shoes, perhaps? I'd be wearing them later when Betty, her Ed, Jim, and I would go to a restaurant—no diving into the bread basket, no overloading my fork—the pumps with Cuban heels, made me taller by an inch and a half, which in the metric system amounted to, er ... er ... "America has much to offer ..." Wait a minute, I had had a movie star before, at the Oostervelds, Freddie Bartholomew on a page from a magazine thumbtacked to the right and above the picture of God decked out as shepherd. Beautiful, this Bartholomew boy, pretty suit, collar of the realest lace, no doubt, Little Lord Fauntleroy, *jajaja.* Dientje made me take him down, Too dangerous, she said, If anyone ever came upstairs they'd wonder who had put that fancy boy up on their wall. I hid him inside the storage bin at the end of the stairs where Johan kept his schoolbooks and the stack of paid bills REMOVED WHEEL FROM MOWING MACHINE, CLEANED IT AND SHORTENED THE BLADE, ONE GUILDER EIGHTY. And where Sini's and my chamberpot lived, before and after use.

"... but we should do so without political conditions, not try to silence those whose ideologies we don't agree with. We need to help those societies help themselves but for it to make any sense at all, private American citizens are going to have to offer it ..."

I had never heard anyone talk like this before, lecture-like, not even at my Teacher's College. Giving me a digest would be just fine, perhaps if I didn't look so enthralled, didn't keep on nodding yesyesyestellmemore ...

Stealthily, my eyes rummaged among the stained-glass panels again for where I had started out in life. If I could locate England, suggestive of a dog sitting up, I'd be close, a sliver of North Sea then. There, Holland. No wonder it kept giving me trouble, look at the size, a dot no bigger than the hole in the side of the shoebox in which Rachel and Sini once made a panorama, cutouts from picture postcards rising up from the glue underneath a ceiling of translucent paper, red, so I too, like the bigger girls on my street, had a box you could peek into and see, tiny houses, little animals in mine, even a goat by a clump of trees, laundry strung between them, knitted shreds hanging from a string. The longer you looked, the more you saw, the vaster it became ...

Did I ever daydream?

Dumbfounded, I looked at him. How did he know that just a second ago I had seen us lie down, heads together on the same pillow, smell of coffee around us—I'd have to learn to make coffee—listening to records, Bach, Piaf, or a gypsy tune, about roses in bloom, music that made you want to move up and down, the way the boat inside the glass dome in my house of birth rocked on waves, the harder you pulled at the string, the wilder it went ...

I followed him out to the street. It was raining again, as earlier that afternoon when we had walked along the Charles River. As then, he opened his umbrella and held it over us. I wanted to squeeze his arm just the tiniest bit as if to say, nice being here with you. "I have them," I said, about daydreams, "only sometimes"—he might think me a bad choice—"you could almost say never."

"Of course you do," he said, "You just won't tell." What he, more than anything else, would like—something he so far hadn't told anyone—was to be one of those private citizens to be sent abroad, to Southeast Asia, preferably. Soon companies would be coming to campus for interviews and he'd be sending out letters to American firms that already did business overseas. Oil, packaged foods, he'd consider it all. "I'll have to learn a lot more than I know now and be trained, which is fine."

Silently, I walked next to him. What was I doing here,

with somebody who'd disappear the minute he got his de-
gree? It had taken a five-hour drive and a lot of sitting, all
the way from Pearl River, with instructions at every mile on
what to do and what never to do—kiss the first time around.
I had even memorized what to say at cocktailtime to show I
knew about drinks, "El Presidente for me, Jim." I didn't even
like liquor. I had to go back too, a ten-hour drive for what
Americans called a blind date?

"Nothing might come of it," I heard him say, "There's
quite a bit of unemployment. Many of the students here, including Ed, are convinced it won't affect us. There aren't
too many MBAs around, they keep on saying, we're highly
salable. But not having any connections and with no money
behind me whatsoever, I'm not sure how long I can wait it
out. I may need to take whatever job I can get. As long as
the eight or ten or twelve hours I'll be devoting to work each
day add up to more than an increase in my or my boss's net
profit figure, I'll be all right. But if that's the only result, if
what I do with my waking hours doesn't benefit those at a
disadvantage, I will have failed."

"Not a chance," Jim, "I have faith in you." If he were not
to leave for some faraway land—just contemplating it was
cheery—if, say, he stayed around, closer to home, I might
be able to see him again, for more walks. It didn't have to be
immediately, I wasn't letting myself get carried away again.
This winter would be fine, or the next or spring, or the one
after that, I could wait ...

From somewhere in the car came the word *funeral* again. As
though it was a pleasant word, to be repeated over and over,
Good morning, *funeral*, Good afternoon, *funeral*, more of
the same and Good night whoever is still around and won't

need one, yet. What if I pushed the wrong kind on him? Like taking advantage of someone totally defenseless. If life had not turned out as he'd hoped, shouldn't he get his way now that it was over? No burial, I guessed, he wouldn't want to be boxed in; maybe in his mind I did that already in the hotel room in Amsterdam. Proving what he may have feared, that I'd commit him to an institution, as his aunt had done to his mother.

I weighed it a little longer, to make as sure as I could I wasn't doing something else wrong. You couldn't undo a mistake like that. "No burial," I whispered at last into the stillness of the car. "He wouldn't have wanted to take up space where children might be able to play."

"It's the right decision," Vinny said. "Cremation then," I offered up, feeling like a turncoat, a supplier to the furnace, like my beautiful cousin who, it was said, sent her own there to save her skin. "Where to scatter?" I asked.

"That's for later," someone hushed.

I knew it could wait. Where, though? Near water, that would be important. The Delaware River? Where life had been idyllic, he claimed; maybe I should honor that, not think of myself for once. No, they shouldn't get him back. That family had had him long enough. I'd choose a new place, with no memory at all, neither his nor ours, where only the sea would hold him ... and if I wasn't brave enough to let go of him myself I'd find someone else. Off Block Island, that would be the site, where we would have gone for our next summer's stay. An unspoiled place, he had called it, wide open still, like the polder he had told Lloyd and Dottie about, where you could imagine another start at life; a better one than what you knew.

Eyes shut again, I flee the Long Island Expressway at half-light and race back to the day we met while I still can. In Ed's room, that's where I stuck out a hand to a blur—I don't see well when I'm nervous. Jim, who asked how the ride up had been, apologized for being late; a report was due. He suggests what we might do, "Go for a walk?" and leaves to change his clothes. It took so long I worried he hadn't liked what he saw, even though Betty had predicted I'd bowl him over. When he finally did return, more apology, same report, the future of irradiated food, he was wearing soldier pants pushed into galoshes furnished by the army too, the good kind, that had liberated. We walked to the Charles River, across from the business school, walls all ivied up, very calming, like the front of Johan's house. I beamed at the leaves still hanging on the vines, curled up some and none too glossy, just as ivy ought to look in winter. Boston's weather could be a lot worse, Jim said, there could be fantastic amounts of snow and slush and it could be really cold. "The same in your country, I believe."

"And dank, Jim, and soggy, frog's country, people say.

"No, I skate not, swim not, no it's not a motto," he made me laugh too, "No, not out of principle and no, no, not a commandment, I cannot do it, I must be a geographical error."

"Are you warm enough, Ann?" he asks, changing my name from Annie, as Betty had introduced me. He had changed his from James to Jim the minute he and his little friends had been out of his mother's earshot: "James is a name for grownups, call me Jim," which he changed to Steve when he got to Yale so no one could confuse him with the other freshman from Durfee Hall, where one evening Idy showed up, suitcase in hand.

"Come, I'm renting us an apartment, James, I cannot live alone. I tried to ignore the landlord and his wife, just as you said, but they keep on loitering below my window and have become so violent they frighten me. Hurry, James, I need you with me before night closes in."

I had been right, he was calling me Ann again. "You're shivering," he says, eyes shiny and very soft, like a little boy in need of sleep. He offers me his scarf and the spot underneath his umbrella. Shouldn't we be going in, we kept saying, this is silly, it's cold and the rain isn't letting up. We keep on walking, back, forth, along the river's edge. In the distance, the outline of a boathouse resembling a pagoda; closer, a lone sculler already training for a future regatta, doing battle, Jim says, pursuing his grail, no matter what.

He says a little more: born here, lived there, flourished here as well as there. Me, too, Jim. And a cat, he said, there was always a cat or a dog or both, and books that got read out loud after dinner, a bowl of apples on the table, a habit he and his mother kept up after the others left home: Arnold Bennett, a beloved author, what about Proust, did I know him? Not really, though, I do read, Jim, good books too, one by somebody French, I forgot his name, who told you practically on page one that she, whoever, did something to her husband that wasn't right, poisoned him, I believe, very exciting and it had a foreword, which I skipped. Such nonsense coming out of my mouth and look what it did, made him laugh. I loved that.

I asked about his family. He answered, not eagerly, as though he'd rather not. A mother still, yes, highly artistic, a father, very much alive too. We both had stepmothers? "Mine is a great cook, too, Jim, makes gooseberry fluff airy as a cloud." And we were both the youngest, another fluke. One sister in his case, who traveled a great deal; you could be sure that each letter came from some other fascinating place. And a brother, Phil, who had had to work hard for his education, dug ditches, carried lumber, anything to pay his way through college. Jim admired him a lot and whereas he himself had merely served, with a pencil, Phil had loved the army; he still went to reserve camp. No, not often in touch, his brother wasn't the type. And back to talking about books again.

When we were first married and living in Detroit, where a job was offered, Jim did more than recommend books, he'd bring them home from the library. "*Old Wives' Tales*, I bet you won't be able to put it down, Ann." "How about *John Brown's Body*, then? about America's past, that book you'll finish, won't you?"

"I'm already getting somewhere with it, Jim, page six coming up." He had probably wanted to discuss at night as he used to, apples embellishing the table, which in his married state were kept in the refrigerator from which he takes one every day. Took.

Straight ahead, Manhattan loomed. It had been fourteen years since I first came to America and cut short any conversation about "my" war. In that one I had merely been a Jew; this time I was convinced I was the one to have done something bad, something shameful. Hush, I thought, you don't want anyone seeing you as the killer? Sitting stockstill, I shook.

Soon I'd be where Jim's death took place, sixteen blocks past the Midtown Tunnel, tiled like a hospital ward, the East River flowing above, then along Second Avenue sidewalks dotted with people going somewhere or having no goal at all but to get through the night, past Kathy's and Julie's school then, where the previous year, after that endless school strike, parents in favor of decentralization urged Jim to run for Parents Association president. "Well-spoken as you are and many decibels less loud than anyone else on our side, you're the only one who can win." He did not win. "It's all right," he said, "I'll get over it." Within the shadow of that building, where he lost his only try for elected office, he had ended his life, in the apartment situated right above the ginkgo tree that would already be showing fruit to be collected in autumn by the Chinese lady who liked to roast them for a feast.

What had Jim been thinking and seeing on his way home? Was his mind made up already, or not until after he woke up? If he had gone to sleep at all, that is. How would I ever know what happened? And even if his note—I'd find it—said, "Long before we met, all my adult life and before, I have been meaning to end it," it could be a lie, to both of us. Still, it would help.

Where were we now, how close to home? I had to get there before Appie could get his paw on that note. He could be playing with it right now, tossing it around, ripping it to shreds; and I wouldn't know what it said. My mouth tight with anxiety, I lifted myself off the seat. Billboards, those I saw, proclaiming the biggest and the best. And there now, the mouth of the tunnel, blood-red taillights marking the way in.

THERE WAS NO MUSIC at his funeral. Music, like compassion, makes me weak. And no rabbi to conduct the service, Jim wasn't that kind of Jew. On the arm of a minister friend with whom he had stood in front of the school to protect the teachers who refused to strike and the children who still came to learn, I entered the room, bit by bit. At a long wooden box, resting on a platform, we halted. I put three roses on top, one from each of us, Kathy, Julie and myself. Then, head bowed again, I sat down next to Sini, one leg at the ready in the aisle for immediately afterward—make it short, Howard, I had asked and nothing God-like, please—and I could go downtown again, home; look some more for a note.

I listened to the eulogy and did not hear. I began to think, of the lie I had told the evening I arrived, then called back, "Was not heart attack, Howard. Was something else." He knew, he said, from the way it had come out. Underneath the trembling of his voice I kept busy rubbing the red, white and blue dots of my blouse, Jim's last gift, four months before, when I turned thirty-seven, the first time I had ever had anything made of silk. I stroked it and took stock of where I might find his letter. He could have hidden it anywhere. I should check the hamper, how could I have forgotten about the hamper? The linen closet, another oversight; sheets, towels, washcloths, pillowcases. Bag with shoe polish and rags, I'd do something about that too, as soon as I got out of here, past friends, past Phil and Jim's sister who, when they saw me a few minutes ago, acted as if nothing had happened, as though they were in town anyway and decided to stop by; which is probably how I presented myself too.

No, I did not take in Howard's words; I kept on stroking and lining up in my head where else I could look for that piece of paper. Could it be in his briefcase? Examined so often already I knew the contents by heart: stacks of graph paper for long-range corporate planning, books on statistical techniques, and a folder, decorated with flowers tall enough to reach the sun, inscribed TO DAD IN THE OFFES, holding Julie's rendering of Charlie Brown and Kathy's opinion of a speech by Martin Luther King Jr. It was good.

The *I Ching* book, I could go through that again too, although so far there had been nothing, no scribble in a margin, no word underlined nor an arrow drawing attention to a hexagram, not even to Number 19, where it is mentioned, when the eighth month is reached, misfortune will befall. My God, maybe it was under my mattress. I ought to lift it instead of sagging onto it as I had for two evenings now in spite of what Carole, Vinny, Lloyd and Dottie said, "Take her into the kids' room with you, Sini."

Sini also could not stop me from being where I imagined

he had been alive last; or just before last. Sprawled across the bed I groped for his warmth, offering mine, moving my mouth and cheek across every thread of pillow muttering over and over again, "We'll fight this." *Bad times don't stay bad, I know, hush, I'm holding you, feel?* It couldn't be tighter. Several times I heard Sini go to the bathroom, pausing at my door first, "Are you all right, Annie?" The sound of toilet flushing then, over which I could still hear her sob, while I, cat close by, waited for a patch of light to creep through the blinds, when I'd get up; to resume the search.

My second foot nudged toward the aisle. In my mind I was already leaving; door, corridor, elevator, lobby, and out again the second I could.

I looked away from what dominated the room, the oblong shape of death, walnut-stained "as selected," and looked toward the ceiling, from which a candelabrum hung, one, two, three, four, five, six arms, I counted, each holding a candle, all casting some form of shadow, denser here, lighter there, from where, suddenly, my mother's face appeared, eyes luminous gray-blue, a little melancholy, just as I remembered them. She wasn't even wearing her headache rag ... how could I be seeing her, here in this dim and dreary room, or anywhere? She was smiling. Had she come to comfort me? Eyes wide open I hung on to her face, which was framed by a mysterious light as a requiem pleads for *Lux perpetua luceat eis Domine.* I heard it although no one was singing, least of all myself.

A sheet of ice sweeps my back. Had she come to get me? Was it now my turn to die? For a second I glanced down and back up again, as afraid of still seeing her as of not seeing her. I should tell her before it's too late that Sini had been doing her schoolwork that time, that I was the one who had nudged the inkpot off the table, something for which Sini got punished. "Go upstairs and stay there, Annie would never have done this," Mother said, giving me a smile I did not deserve.

I had another memory, a better one, of her smiling, when I'd skip alongside her on our way to the synagogue where, at Simchas Torah, when the last portion of the Fifth Book of Moses was read and the beginning of the First Book again, they gave out candies, Sweets of the Bride, hard on the outside but juicy when you bit through. On regular Saturdays I got something there too, a penny that smelled of cologne, like my grandmother and the bag she fished it from, after I had gotten through prettifying her hair and pushed those wayward strands into wings, mainly up.

I can see it all now, the ark, the men underneath prayer shawls in shades of black and dirty-white, talking cattle, the business most of them were in. Not Jopie; he does not join their chatter. Having to work in Father's butcher shop is bad enough, he says, especially in early spring, when other boys his age were outside trying to impress the girls with this feat or that and he could be seen prodding a cow through the streets, oranges decorating her horns for this, a last appearance. He has been given strict instructions, how to ring bells. "Not as if it's intimate, Jopie, or you're afraid to disturb," and how to say, just as loud, "What part of this beauty would you like for your Easter dinner?"

"He's no salesman," my father complains, when Jopie returns, order book mostly blank. "What'll be with him, at this rate he'll end up like Mozes here," whose body enthusiastically keeps on shaking in front of the ark. "He wouldn't have a cent if it weren't for the money he worms out of me and his other brothers."

I know I am not inside a synagogue but in the proper room for remembering my husband, and that what I've been looking up at is no more than an ordinary ceiling, some paint, some shadows cast by a fantasy lamp, not at all what showed before, so real I could almost touch. Perhaps I had not lost those I loved, not completely. Their bodies, yes, they were gone, but something else, whatever you call it, soul, atmosphere, that stays. Would I, in spite of the hurt, also carry Jim with me for the rest of my life? He probably expected me to. He all but hinted at that when he asked me to marry him. No, not asked, not directly, that too was more of a hint, dropped at the very end of my weekend in Detroit, and all the way back to Pearl River I kept wondering, did he propose or not? He did, apparently; I was already engaged. His mother, who didn't even know I existed, said so in a letter, "What a shock."

I threw another glance at the casket. As long as it was still standing there it seemed less lonely. You'd almost wish Howard would keep on talking. "The pain of loss," he just said. "The tragedy to Jim's family."

I rubbed, harder now, same sleeve, my watch, time not going anywhere, not fast enough I saw; and both wedding bands on my hand, Vinny had given me Jim's, a double pledge to my children. Again I wondered whether he had kept his on or removed it beforehand, keeping our marriage intact as long as possible. Or was that a wish I clung to like the note I might never find and would have to learn to live without. Maybe just as well, being able to read, and reread his words might torment me more than my own words did.

"It's not you I don't trust, Jim," I had said once again, just two weeks ago, along the North Sea that time, the same don't-be-upset-with-me prattle I trotted out whenever he suggested, "Let me teach you to swim."

I know you won't drop me, it's all that water I fear, I need to feel ground or I panic.

Sini might have the answer. She's sitting right next to me, Jim, pinky firmly anchored in her mouth. I told you about that habit, didn't I? Sini might know, having been the one who, on summer afternoons, had to take me to the pool, Mother's orders issued from the sofa. Had she, if only for a second, checked on her friends who were having all that fun in the deep end and left me to bob around alone? Or had my fear begun way before, on the night I stumbled down the birth canal with Mother's warning in my ears, "Watch out for fluids from now on," except for the weekly washpail she'd put me in so I'd smell good for the onset of shabbas.

I may never have trusted anyone, Jim, completely, a realization that has come to feel brand new. Perhaps you were only teasing, Johan, when you'd say, "Hope the soldiers won't sneak up on us tonight, girls, I don't know what I'll do." But what about Dientje. "How much longer do we have to keep 'm, Johan? It's too dangerous." And I, in their bed, would make myself as small as possible so that I was almost not there already, and I'd stick a leg across the brink to complete the picture.

That's it, I thought, when Jim found work in Detroit, I'll never see him again; our towns are too far apart. "I'll write," he promised, when he stopped off in Pearl River to say good bye, "America has a fine postal system, Ann, let's use it." "What would it be like to see a city with the heart of the auto industry in it, Jim, I always wondered," I lied. As a matter of fact, I've been curious ever since I saw the picture of an assembly line in my English book; it looked intriguing. "Why don't you come visit," he said, "the Fourth of July, say, the long weekend of Independence Day, which," he said then, or later when our marriage rose up from a sea of thisses and thats, "ought to be called Interdepen-

dence Day, a great idea Ann, but one already thought of by
FDR."

He wasn't at the airport, Willow Run. I waited, then waited twice that long. He knew when I'd arrive; "Till tomorrow,"
we had said on the phone, "Looking forward to it, Ann."
Traffic, of course, a lot of it, in this here Detroit, or trouble
with the borrowed car. I should just sit and read some more
so I'd have plenty to say when I saw him. I opened *Time*
magazine—my very own subscription—and turned to the
business page. Statistics looked somewhat brighter, zigzags
pointing up, sharply too here and there, the way I cut my
nails, which Betty disapproved of but I liked—that's how Sini
did hers, never stopped men from flocking to her. Car sales
looked favorable too. No wonder he couldn't get to the airport, the answer was right here on paper. I kept on turning
pages. This magazine discussed everything, look, something
about a marriage bed, it ought to be placed in a north-south
position apparently, in tune with magnetic currents, spelled
with an *e*; the other kind, hmm, Rachel would put in a pan-
cake when it got to be my birthday, several currants for
mouth, nose, a cluster for eyes … I looked up and around.
Was that him? Crew cut and loose-limbed kind of walk? Or
was it a case of *trompe l'oeil* as I had seen, in which museum
again, the Frick? The Metropolitan? Who could remember?
Jim kept writing about so many, "all fabulous institutions,
Ann, go have a look." I was lucky there had been a fire at
MoMA or I would have felt compelled to go there too … I had
never given my education a thought before. I was getting
somewhere, though, especially in the kitchen. Last time I
made a cheesecake it was only the tiniest bit runny and I no
longer poured a bottle of wine in a pan, added a chicken, and
yelled, "Here she is, coq au vin."

Flustered, I ruffled through the magazine again. Every picture seemed to have two people in it, whether it was of pots and pans, a deodorized armpit, or a pool in front of a motel, even a girl taking a laxative had a man beaming in the background.

The terminal had completely emptied out. I could become obsolete, waiting around like last year's model car, left in a lot. I should do something, go to the counter, check when the next plane would return, or call, a little less drastic. What was his number, though? Something with an eight and a zero, the rest I forgot, same with my own number. The only one I could summon up was my father's, which I hadn't dialed for a couple of years. Wait, it was coming back, quick, over to the wall before it left me again.

"How awful" he said it would have been had I gone back to Pearl River? He had wanted to straighten his room, began with a drawer but obviously more time had gone by than he had realized, he'd be over in thirty minutes. Odd, I thought, to have gotten so carried away with a cleanup job.

But when I got there, his room was not neat at all, least of all that drawer, half of what should've been inside, socks and underwear, was either hanging over the edge or lying in a heap in front of it, along with a pile of records. "Beethovens I see, Jim, the same symphonies I own, what a coincidence." Had he joined RCA as well? "Yes-yes, same with me, I love music, got that from my mother, I guess."

There was a lot of music that July Fourth weekend. Some I never knew was music, scratchy noises I thought hitherto— an elegant word Jim taught me, or was it heretofore?—and I would've turned them off, it could have been Stravinsky I had done that to or Britten's "O Rose Thou Art Sick": or Dame Edith Sitwell reeling off ditties, her definitely, "Do Not

Take a Bath in Jordan, Gordon." "How does her tongue do it, Jim?" was the best I could come up with.

Some he played himself on his recorder bought in Paris, a little waltz? Yes, I tried it out, "Watch it, Ann, don't trip over my shoes, careful," until I nudged them out of the way, under his bed, *allez allons*. There was even more music than that, left-wing songs from the Spanish Civil War, Irish songs, songs of democracy, and Marlene Dietrich. Sitting on the floor, our backs against the side of his bed we listened to her, *Sehnsuchtlieder*, Jim called them, Songs of Desire. Of parting and waiting, I said. "She came back to Europe when there wasn't much to sing about, except for that."

Still drooped in a chair in the room where I had requested no music or flowers, I could, if I dared look, see friends, I knew they were there, arranged in pairs, I imagined, two by two with pity in their eyes that I could not bear. And Phil was there, and Lucy, not Bob. I wondered whether he'd ever come to New York and visit; if only for the children. Or would he also find that too painful?

I rubbed the other sleeve, with its red and white and blue dots, the colors of both flags, my old one and the one that had adopted me. I made it mine much more than I ever would have thought.

On Friday I am going back, Jim, to pick up Kathy and Julie. "Why don't you stay in Holland?" Sini keeps saying. "You can do that now, the children will adjust, they're still so young"—as if I didn't know. "Come live in Scheveningen," she suggests, where she can keep an eye on us, "or in The Hague, where they have an American school." Even if I could afford that school I'm not sure I would live in Holland; the kids would fight me if I took them away. This country is really theirs, not something they acquired, and I myself would have trouble leaving the place where you and I made a life. Besides, I've never been good at pulling up voluntarily, so what am I thinking?

First thing after the funeral I would call the kids: "Did you have a good time at the fair?" My stepmother had asked a friend, whose English offered more than "cookie" and "give kiss," take them. "Mommy's coming back in just a few days, get you ready for school. I, *er*, even Appie misses you."

I had already called the potter Jim gave a tour of the city to, his name and number found on an index card inside the gray metal box I had emptied—looking for the note. I had to tell him what happened, of course, or I would've made no sense.

"You never saw my husband before, Brian—still, did you notice anything off?"

It did seem strange, now that he reflected on it, that when they had rested in a small garden with a waterfall flowing down, sipping a soft drink, a cop came up to a girl and told her not to lean on the ivy growing on the wall and Jim had laughed, "Such concern for a plant ..."

Sini's probably right, Jim, life might be easier in Holland. But what if it doesn't work out? We can't very well run back and forth across the ocean: Where to next? Which way now? As soon as I've decided, over here, I doubt myself again, over there? I know I'm the only one in charge now, still I wonder what you'd say, something I should, of course, wean myself from. Not today. There's time for that, there's time for everything in this room, where even a short eulogy won't end ...

Detroit was the city where I learned to say "I love you," at first mumbling it into his neck, until I could say it loudly and look at him too, with Jim responding in a number of languages, including that of his grandparents, *ja tebia lublu*, the Russian "love you" his mother sometimes used.

Only hours before I left Detroit after the visit I had whee-dled an invitation to, he had not said a word, about a future, a commitment, or even that we'd see each other again. Un-less it was stuffed inside his stepmother's cooking, which he said I'd love. The same with the dinner conversations around her and Bob's dining room table, especially if Phil was there too, and their sister had stopped off to or from some exotic place—in which case the sparks would fly.

He would not have needed words to propose. He could have just swung out an arm when, on our way to the res-taurant for my send-off, we had to wait for a light alongside a coffee shop where our names were linked on the window, Jimmy's and Ann's, very jaunty, with curlicues, somewhat dusty, true, but a little water, few drops of vinegar, and a chamois would have spruced us up nicely. Jim did not see, he was talking about Italy, where he had traveled during his stay in France. Those crazy Italians he had met, "their moods going up and down, fine for opera, but you wouldn't want to be around them on a day-to-day basis."

Could I be the one to point it out? Look to your right, I could say, just past me, "Can't get rid of the us, I guess." Would he think me pushy, the way he had found the British at times? If I did it quickly? Already his hand was fumbling with the gearshift and we began to edge forward. There was something he wanted to check with me, he said, there was a Volkswagen, seemingly in good shape, he was thinking of buying. What did I, considering my background, think of that? "Do it," I shouted, eyes lingering over as much of the sign as still showed, only the Jimmy part ...

"It was yellow, though, is that okay for a car, Ann?"

"Isn't the motor more important?" It didn't come out as a question, more like an accusation, but only one letter was left of what could have been. Then even the *J* of the restaurant sign disappeared. He loved my sense of practicality, he said, as we drove off for real. Next week he'd look at that VW again.

The streets were nearly deserted, a few children stepping as if on parade, an elderly woman herding them back into the house. In the business district some people looking into windows, none at the store Jim worked at, in spite of the fact that five new styles of skirts were on display. He didn't seem to see that any more than our names united at the coffee shop. He had crossed the Channel again and was back in England, discussing bowlers, umbrellas and the Underground system, big red worms, with padded seats, in long tunnels.

Slowly we drove along the boulevard that would take us to the Detroit River and the restaurant for the farewell. Would it rain again, I wondered, as it did when I had arrived? And would Betty be picking me up for the drive home? "Tell me everything," she'd say, "from beginning to end. You didn't let him get away, did you?"

I looked out the window. I should at least try to memorize some of where we were, so that I could make the weekend glisten again long after it was gone.

Behind me, or still coming up, was the park with the bandshell where we had sat on grass still damp from a shower, and listened while march after march tore into the air, no boots had swamped my mind, I only heard music played with vigor and Jim's hand tapping time on his knee.

Way off, I couldn't see it yet, Belle Isle, where we had watched the fireworks and he held me when I shook: "It's nothing, Jim," but those noises, those whistle-thud-claps, a bomb? I had to get away before the flames reached us. Where were my father, mother, and Jim, where was he? Still holding, asking no questions, as if he sensed something I had never said.

He stopped the car. This is where he wanted to come, he said, to the restaurant closest to the river. I got out. Jim drove to where he could park. An iron carrier went by, then a barge, and a riverboat that hooted. The air was heavy. Clouds were building up and spreading. Again I counted the number of ships, three, the one still blasting. Three toots, when I came to this country, meant we were about to pass another boat you could spot if you looked up from the railing. It could've been Jim's, on his way to France, we could've passed each other halfway. They had served herring and pea soup on mine and played the Dutch national anthem, which had made swallowing hard, while Jim, on his boat, told himself, *Stop your gorging, no more cheese, ice cream and petits fours on your plate, You only have one suit.* He wore it that evening, gray with a hint of stripe, a darker one on his tie. His shirt was white and buttoned down. Near the collar, the tiniest of birthmarks. I had kissed it.

Across from where I stood was Canada. We had gone there too, so I could say, not only have I been to Michigan but abroad as well. Had we taken a tunnel? Things were already becoming vague ... a coffee, and we had danced, sort of, when looking for a picnic spot along a dirt road, to music escaping through a window, "It better be a foxtrot, Ann, since that's what I think we're doing."

He was whistling when he came back, a Piaf song; one more memory to add. Together we watched whatever traffic moved along the river. "There's always water where we are, Jim. Remember the Charles River, where we stood six months ago?" "I was so happy I had no umbrella," he said, it had given him the excuse to walk close.

"You offered me your arm, Jim, and your scarf, which you kept rearranging around my neck." Another excuse, he said, to touch. He was shocked when he first saw me, he could own up to that now. Of "Nordic charm" Ed had told him, and there I was, dark and small. "Your eyes got to me. Drowned in a pool of green," I scribbled down that night, crossed out and entered again in the margin of a paper I was trying to finish up. "And your accent, that too I loved right away, it sounded Irish to me."

"I shouldn't be having an accent at all, Jim, not any more."

"Don't get rid of it," he looked worried.

"How could I? I don't even hear that I have any."

In that case, he thought, there was hope.

I too began to hope again. He said he was sorry he'd never been to Holland. "Pretty country, Jim." It was better to know a few places well than many badly, he decided. Maybe that too could be remedied someday, "It's never too late, Jim," I said, beaming, as he hoped to get back to Paris and visit Madame Giraud, his landlady who had thought of him as her son. Every time there was something new in his life he let her know, as when he got the job at the department store. Maybe they'll open up a branch in Paris, she wrote back. "Who knows, Ann, maybe it'll grow …" For years "Meet me under the clock" meant only one thing in Detroit, underneath the clock above Kern's main door, and then they'd be off to the competitor, "but now people are wandering into our store as well." "That's hopeful, Jim." And they were planning to throw a big party for their seventy-sixth anniversary. "Now then, if they have money for that, they can't be in too bad a shape." "Maybe." He sounded doubtful. "Old habits are hard to change, many of the salesladies are still wearing carpet slippers, that hardly attracts young customers." "Don't worry about it, Jim, it'll work out and if it doesn't here, something else will come up. Sometimes," I gazed up at him, "things don't come as fast as we'd like, I know about that." Maybe he had heard, but he wasn't done with Paris yet. He'd be sure to return to Le Tour d'Argent, where they gave you a card with the number of your duck written on top, LE NUMERO DE VOTRE CANARD, 358.801, his had been, "a superb meal," a grand finale to a year more special than any he had ever known. From his table he had been able to catch a glimpse of the Seine and Notre Dame, although something had been missing. In that romantic city, that city of love, he had never had a girlfriend. He had sat there by himself that night.

He took my arm. "We need to go in," he said, pointing to the restaurant. "All during your visit I have been thinking about this, to bring you here on this historic weekend, the birth of our nation, and put our own crown on it. One hundred eighty-two years ago ..."

Betty had almost predicted something like this, "Don't expect him to say, 'Hi-hi, honey, marry me,'" like on the farm. High-minded people might present it as part of an essay, potentially it could be an essay of its own; I just had to be clever enough to know what passage counted or in which maze it was concealed. Ann Reiss ... it had a nice sound to it, especially if you hung on the to *R* for a while, turning it into the roar of a lion ... I'd be marrying into this brilliant family, painting, journalisting, building bridges ... isn't that what Phil did? Even in their spare time they probably had nothing but weighty thoughts. In my letter home I'd better say something about the name, though, "It's not German, Father, although it looks that way, it used to be Russian and very long." He's Jewish, I'd be sure to add, they didn't have to know he had never been bar mizvahed.

"Our crown." The rest of the proposal, the more specific lines, he was probably saving for later. I should start teaching him some Dutch, so he and my father could have a real conversation, anatomy of a cow maybe, and what could go wrong with it, mouth and hoof soreness. What was the other illness called again? The one udders used to get ...

"... after a long war with Great Britain ..." I quickly nodded. Heh? What war? I'd also better apply myself to the sex book on Betty's shelf again, bungling methods could have lamentable consequences, it warned, but it showed nothing useful, no positions or anything, just side- and front-views of organs, mine I didn't recognize and the male one all loops and lines that would both get wider and longer at a certain point—which point they kept under wraps—but was already four inches, I had put the measuring tape on top and if you thought about it in centimeters and started the multiplying ...times 2 1/2, no, worse, times 2.540 ...

I quickly devoted myself to Jim's presentation again, the escalating war with Britain, American Revolution, Founding Fathers, and the fancy handwriting on "our most important historical document, Ann." I tried to remember what I had learned about it at the Americanization course at Pearl River High School, faded-curtain-dented-vase, I might not have been listening when the teacher got to why there'd be no mail delivery and offices would be closed. Day-off-day-off, was all

I heard, thrilled. Had to do with a Tea Party? Which wasn't a party at all, the tea got dumped into a harbor somewhere. "So much peetee," Françoise said, turning it into a rhyme.

Just a second, the Fourth of July was watermelon day, seeds and all, hot dogs and fireworks, a parade, flags dangling everywhere. Jim did say why, but what, exactly, had passed me by again. As though history was of no interest to me, except, perhaps, my own. And not too much of that either.

THE RESTAURANT in which getting married was and wasn't mentioned was French. At least they tried to give you that impression, Jim said, with cartoons on the brick walls and sketches of nudes dimly lit. The lady nearest where I sat had kept something on, a hat and a ribbon that dangled between her breasts. Her partner inside the frame was not totally bare either, a closed umbrella sat clasped between his legs.

The candle got lit, the menus handed out.

I looked for something cheap, he had spent so much money on me already, breakfasts out, lunches out, dinners …

"I hope you'll have the duck too," he said. "It's supposed to be good."

Instantly jealous, I wondered, had he been here before—and with whom.

He ordered wine, a white Bordeaux, as he had drunk

on his last night in France. The waiter stepped back. Jim leaned forward.

Our hands maneuvered toward each other around the candle that burned darkly near the wick, then shot up in a thin point of yellow that wavered, tilting to the left, right, until I saw an entire row of lights, as when we used to celebrate the Miracle of Chanukah.

"That we managed to meet, Ann, and here, not in Europe, I still marvel at it. When I landed in Cherbourg, you, I believe, were about to spot the Ambrose Lightship."

It was five in the morning. I was still in my bunk. America won't go away, I thought, I'll see it later, but my cabin mate wouldn't let me, "Geddupennie, we're home," which of course, I wasn't, not yet I mean, not quite ... I turned my eyes back to the flame, it still fluttered.

"I know it's not easy," he said, "to be in a place where the language isn't yours and where, once the strangeness wears off, life acquires a sort of gray quality. You need to force yourself to enter into some of the richness around you, a state comparable, perhaps," he hesitated, "to falling in love, say, and suddenly everything appears different."

"Yes," was all I could think of to say. I looked into his face. Never had I met anyone as special, as warm and soulful. I would cherish that. Life would be good, better than good. I'd make sure of it. Under the same roof ... and not just for three nights as now, but in the same bedroom even, together, where you sleep and get up, of course.

I looked away, not wanting him to see my eyes, roaring with fear, not very festive, but how, a thought coming a little late, perhaps, considering our joined future was almost here, but how could you hang on to feeling good about each other, my mother surely lost that; so did my father, for that matter. How could you stop your mouth from sliding into a whine or making a remark that bit? What does it mean to love? To love enough, that is. Wishing someone well, one of the girls in my rooming house said. Isn't that what you say to a person who goes away? And you won't get to see again, as in a bad dream, all at once you're on a piece of road, you recognize it, every cobblestone, every unevenness in the pavement, careful. You run, past trees many times taller than you are and by houses just the right height to look into, not in this dream where you keep on racing after something or someone you cannot reach no matter how you speed. How could I be so close to happiness tonight and feeling everything else at the same time? All those ups and downs, like those crazy Italians he had mentioned, "Fine for opera, Ann, but who could live with them?"

Before, though, he had been talking about us, hadn't he? Joyous, momentous, and what about the crown? It was hard to know, "Independence Day," he just said, or said again, which should have been named this, that or the other, Interdependence. "The benefit of this name change could be far-reaching ..." Might there be something in this? I wondered, a little trot before he leaped?

"It would greatly outweigh narrow national interests. Nations cannot go their own way entirely ..."

"They shouldn't, Jim." It was the same with liberation, I comforted myself, it didn't come and didn't come, until the friendly tanks arrived. Was he always so convoluted, though, or just tonight? Talking on about a day that wouldn't return for an entire year. I had to catch a plane that left a lot sooner than that.

The waiter was back, poured wine, and left again.

Jim raised his glass.

Maybe now it's coming, I thought, the will-you-be-with-me-forever part.

I had read about that combination in a book: candlelight and a glass of wine and she hadn't known what to do first, sip or say yes.

"Santé," I heard.

"Santé," I said. I examined my glass and wiped at a tiny stain my mouth had left on the rim. He could also say it after the wine, I took a quick sip, after the duck or not until we got to the end of the meal, over a sliver of pie and coffee. I had seen that too on a page, in the kind of novel sophisticated Dutch refer to as "kitchenmaid's lit"—he'd kiss her hand, she his? Anyway, hands got kissed, a ring produced, they'd look deep into each other's eyes and off they strode, into the blood-red sunset, which they looked at until everything around them had dimmed.

I spread the napkin on my lap and waited. Easy now, I urged myself, when the duck arrived. In your hurry to get to the coffee part and the beauty around it, you might be stuck with hiccups and not be able to gracefully accept.

Why was he talking about Queen Victoria and Prince Albert now? What did those two have to do with us? "I heard about them," I said quickly, "1837 to 1901." The only thing popping back up from a history book and the only thing I cared to know, the sooner we got rid of them, the better.

I took an entire mouthful of duck, barely bothered to chew.

A whole age was named after this Victoria woman, I just found out.

"A sort of cookie, too, in Holland anyway, plain dry, good for dieting. Dientje once tried. 'If one cookie makes you lose weight,' she said, 'give me twenty...'"

The age itself then was discussed, the architecture which he found ornate, and the furniture, overdone.

If I looked at him much longer I'd cry and I wouldn't even know why. I wished I could think of something else to make him laugh, he had begun to look so tense again, or that I could cradle him in my arms, as un-grown-up as that might seem.

All this good candlelight, wasted on what, the history of England? "Many changes took place there: economic, social, political. Life, however, was confining, especially for women. You should read some of the literature of that time, Thomas Hardy, the Brontë sisters." He seemed to wonder where to go next.

"Yes, Jim." I repeated it. "Yes."

They were a good combination, Albert and the queen, she the sovereign, he her protector and teacher, whose judgment she trusted, even about her clothing. He had many interests, science, industry, the arts. They had a museum named after them, the Victoria and Albert.

"I've been there. A great place." He paused again. "You too might want to visit someday."

I nodded, more emphatically then, as I finished inspecting my duck, yes, I was looking at a genuine carcass. My father would be proud of me, *You got it all,* he'd pronounce, something you couldn't say about Jim's. Too bad I didn't dare ask for his wing—scarcely touched—it would only go back to the kitchen where someone else would do the gnawing, might just as well have been me.

Those others he was bringing in now, Disraeli, Gladstone, Tories and Whigs with or without an *h*, what were they doing in my future? Interrupt him, Betty would say, "I'm beginning to wonder, Jim, why you can't come out with it. Is there a problem?"

"Not that you don't have one, Annie," when he mentioned that museum just now. Why didn't he say: "Will you take me there?" I'd love to consider it.

After the engagement ring, of course, and, adamantly, don't let him offer something dinky; "it needs two stones on either side"—side of what, I had not dared ask. "The trouble with you, Annie, is that you need everything spelled out. Real life isn't like that."

I lifted my wine again, wishing it were milk. Suddenly I remembered our Passover table, set with dishes used only once each year and the special cloth, matzos around the edge, embroidered by Mother's hands. It clearly is a different evening, there's extra wine on the table, for Elijah, although he never comes. "Must've gone to where there was more in his glass than the few drops we've allotted him," Rachel says. Or maybe—my opinion—he's afraid of our yard, a bee could easily have flown over from the neighbor's hives, or he might not want to meet up with old van der Wal, the other neighbor who could be sticking his something through the wire fence again, right along our rosebush that has thorns, his *schlemazzel*, Sini calls it, which some people will tell you means misfortune but she and Aunt Rose, who lifted her skirt in Amsterdam for a living, swore could mean the opposite as well. "At least I'm getting paid for it," she always said, laughing loudly. I'm not allowed to hear that either. "Go play," Mother urges, whenever that aunt visits, "Out, quick, into the backyard." I have a jar in my that hand I keep dipping into the rain barrel until I catch a tadpole. I like to watch it grow fatter, get legs, something else Mothers says "Bah" to.

The image of my backyard melts into the grass strip alongside Johan's and Dientje's outhouse, where the sheets and sanitary napkins that had resisted soaking and boiling were bleached by the sun, showing that anything could be accomplished if you kept on trying.

Long after the sugar had dissolved, I still stirred my coffee, still hoping he'd say it. He surely was wordy, even if you heard only some, it was a lot. You almost had to feel pity for that candle, dripping itself into a puddle of wax—for nothing. Parliamentary Acts he was now adding to the stack. I'd be embarrassed to tell anyone, This is what he came up with. Imagine being married to him, you could be calling out, "Breakfast is getting cold" and he'd still be, whatever, eruditing. Acts ... plural, yet. Who knew how many there were? All needing to be scrutinized. Once that man was on to something he wouldn't let go.

I wriggled my feet out of the Cuban pumps; those shoes pinched. Face as serene as possible, I glanced over to the nearest piece of wall, where the couple in their makeshift fig leaves still stoically stared from their frame. "Nothing can penetrate them," Jim had said when we first sat down. "Neither happiness nor pain—an admirable philosophy."

They'd never have to be in a hurry either. I peeked at my watch. Barely any time left, I had to make that plane, get to work tomorrow. I'd been promoted, Clerk B, eighty-one dollars plus ten cents a week! They had even given me an extra day off, and look how I was paying them back, by sitting as though I had all the time in the world.

Resolutely I finished my coffee.

"Crowning." Who was I to kid myself; it would be like fantasizing I could sing like Piaf because we were the same height. What on earth made me believe I'd become his wife? He didn't say that, he hadn't said anything vaguely like it. I'd get over him, couple of weeks, months at most, you couldn't miss what you never had.

It would be a pity, though, to go back to Pearl River with just a July Fourth story, there was a parade, then something else, a dinner party which was no more than that, dinner. Dessert. And talk about all the wrong things.

Carefully, I focused my eyes on Jim's face again. I did like him. More than liked. There was nothing vulgar about him, no tasteless jokes, no grabbing in the dark, none of what you wouldn't want. Except, of course, for sticking on the wrong topic. But still charming, even now, rhapsodizing about, what, that awful couple again? Yes, Albert this, Victoria that.

Inseparable, he called them. I swallowed. Didn't he know that life was all about people leaving? Dead or not, they left. Before the end of the year Betty would be gone, back to the South. "We're getting married," she'd tell her Ed, whether he wanted to or not, "so I can help you amount to something." I'd miss her. She'd been more than a housemate, more than a friend even, a sister. No more ending my day in her living room for a chat and hear her wish me, "Goodnight, sweet dreams, and all those good things."

Shortly afterwards the other two girls would leave, grad school for the one, another try in the convent for the other; I'd miss them too. After a while new housemates would arrive, followed by another batch. Of course, I'd be fine, no need to remind myself of that, there was the job, typing class, shorthand class, a few seconds' worth of trying to hula-hoop in the backyard—that at least Betty had been bad at. To my very own room then, small, you might say, but it had everything you'd want, bookstand and table, wrought iron, from the store for Gracious Living; a bed, of course, and a chair I'd sit in, listening to Beethoven's symphonies, same nine Jim had, *Time* magazine on my lap, where every ad would evoke "bridegroom" even after being convinced there wasn't going to be one.

I pricked up my ears, concentrated hard. He seemed to be on to something entirely new. "She was badly educated," he said. Who? The queen was? Fit me, too. I lifted my cup up again, whether empty or not. "And short," he added, "barely five feet tall." That's what I was without those uncomfortable pumps, five feet. "But with a towering zest for life," he continued. And she had beautiful eyes. Did I hear him say green? Last time I looked, mine were too, it said so on my passport—no that was gray-green. Well, ash blond was blond, wasn't it, and when people talked about carroty hair didn't they mean ... If I wasn't that queen we surely had an awful lot in common, Victoria and I. If I told Rachel and Sini that I was royal, more or less, they'd moo, to remind me where I was from. Would that make Jim Albert? This was worse than eruditing, this was talking in riddles. Couldn't he express himself so I could understand? Maybe this was the maze Betty had talked about.

"She," Jim now said, "asked him to be her husband."

Why was he waiting? Was I supposed to add the "Will you?" which was probably not at all what a queen says. Some blunder if I did have the courage to ask and had was wrong, about my being her. I was losing all notion of what was real and what wasn't. He was too much for me, or I not enough for him, probably the same, or not, I was beginning to doubt everything, even that I loved-liked-and-didn't. "Crowning"... that's what you went to the dentist for when you cracked a tooth.

I put my cup down, this time for good.

He took my hands, instantly making me forget I was about to hate him forever.

"There was a profound love between them," he went on, "a commitment so great it did not end with Albert's death, at an early age, he had caught something, typhoid fever he wasn't able to shake, his health shot, perhaps, overworked, depressed, or simply because some people are better at fighting off death than others, but whatever the reason, Victoria never stopped loving him. Wasn't that beautiful?"

"I like it," I answered, not exactly sure to what, "I like it very much."

"That's settled then," he said, "You'll be the shortest member of my family. Shall we say in six months?"

Now that his mother was finally in good shape, her anxiety under control, her emotions back in check, she could live alone again, and had he told me she had been studying Braille? So she could not only read to the blind but help them read for themselves too; in short, with her doing well he felt comfortable planning his life and having a wife of his own. "There isn't much I can offer you yet but you will always have whatever I have to give. You'll start with my love."

"That is everything," I said.

WHERE AM I? Still sitting. Not in church; I only go when my choir performs and Jim attends with our little girls. And not in synagogue, that was years ago, nestled in between my mother and her mother who cooed that once I grew up, with fingers like mine, I could easily find work as a hairdresser.

The curtains are drawn where I sit, my heels are half-way off the rug, which is wilted, like the flower patterns on it. Howard's shoes are planted on top, pants navy-blue and creased, same ones he wears on Sundays, perhaps, jacket to match and a shirt from which a face and voice rise, express-ing more feeling than I can take. Father manages to slide in. Husband. Untimely.

So bone-chilling cold in this Reposing Room.

What I would do for a hot-water bottle. I wouldn't know where to start applying it first. Between my hands? Or have it travel up and down and up again, to the back of my neck?

I had a hot-water bottle as a kid, wrapped inside a crocheted jacket to protect from too much heat, and in my wartime bed there was one. On nights when ice flowers patterned the windows, Dientje would put it in my space first, from where Johan tried to get it over to his side, Dientje protesting, "Stop moving those feet around, Johan, Annie here doesn't like all that thrashing about either." But she was doing the same, and I'd spin myself inside a fistful of sheet to keep away from what alarmed and excited and didn't, their nightclothes, bulging in spots.

Even my hands have fallen still, frozen onto my lap. I should make fists, blow into them as on a winter's day, turn them warm and coppery, the color of summer and of my mother's wedding band, which I had wanted to wear when I married. Father gave it to me when I came for the one-year stay that stretched on. "Maybe it can be de-scratched," I wrote to Jim in one of my letters to Detroit. "I would sort of very much like that unless you mind." He did; he wanted to begin with a new slate, as he'd said in a poem the summer he got to live with his father:

a golden dawn / a bird greeting it / I hear the thunder / but far off...

I cringed, stung by Howard's voice deepening with each word, "Loved his wife and children, but more than that he was devoted to the human family and all children ..."

The school strike came back. Those nightly meetings on how to maintain classes and I resenting that he suddenly had the time. It wasn't hard to start hating yourself, was it? My mind wandered next to Amsterdam, the leather jacket I had talked him out of, "Since it isn't for the office, Jim, it doesn't make much sense. Once we're back in New York, how much leisure time will you have?" "That would change," he said. "As soon as the insurance venture stops being a venture, other people will be added, they won't expect me to keep on working eighty hours a week? It's not humanly possible, Ann, they must know that." "I hope so," I said, as unconvinced as he seemed sure. I felt guilty for having spoiled his joy; the jacket did look good on him.

"Buy it, Jim. Do it, please." He kept on wavering, might be a waste, on the other hand, but what if ... When we finally left the shop, without, he apologized to the salesman for having taken up so much of his time.

We journeyed on, across and around canals, fast, as if somebody were after us, lingering only for another I-adore-you-Ann, one more embrace, it began to scare and bewilder me, as though he was the one who had done something wrong instead of me, which I now could only whisper to a lidded box. I tried to slip away from his arms then, people must be watching, I thought. "Let's stop for coffee, or a slice of cake, the kind filled with ginger?" He wouldn't. Past the Royal Palace, first time around, or again, and the National Monument, where a handful of junkies sat around stoned, staring into melon peel as though all the answers could be found there. "Stupid," Jim said, as we rushed past. "Why ruin your brain?" On we pressed, Herengracht, Keizersgracht, Prinsengracht, other canals I had no name for, over to the Rijksmuseum, for a look at Rembrandt's *The Night Watch*, the picture of citizen soldiers getting ready to defy the enemy, something he had taken me for, that same night, in the hotel.

Blearily, I looked up at the ceiling of this particular mourning site, at the miracle lamp, the candelabrum that a while ago, out of the shadows, had made people come back with such clarity I could feel myself being held. It was barely giving off enough light now to make sense of where I was.

It might not have ended badly at all. Giving up hope was so easy; he had turned up when it was darker than this. Take the evening of the big blackout: I thought he'd have to spend the night in the office. Hours later the door opened and there he stood, energized by the long walk home. Maybe it could still happen, even now, when it really mattered.

Listen. The elevator in my building just creaked; it does that when it opens. I don't think it's a dream. And if it is, let me keep it. Footsteps then, his, approaching my door. I jump up, face ready to be kissed. "All day long," he'll say, "I've looked forward to this, to be back with my family"—which he never thought he'd have. First the briefcase comes in, heavy with work for after the meal and before bed. "Are the kids still awake?" he asks, and "What are we eating?" although that he doesn't want an answer to, he likes to be surprised. He tiptoes into Kathy's and Julie's room, kisses them whether they're asleep or not, and sings the lullaby, the same one his mother, wayway back, sang to him, about peace, "May it attend thee through the night."

Inside our bedroom the coins come out of his pocket. He always puts them in the same place, on the dresser with the mirror where often we stand, he with his arms entwined around my body. We look beautiful together, he says. I do look, but quickly, why I don't quite understand unless it's because bits of another face might show, the hollow cheeks of Johan, my father-in-hiding, his hair pointing upward, or his eyes implying I was old enough now to owe him something, what I cannot possibly think about. I turn around and push my face into Jim's chest where the hair is soft, unlike the stubbles on his head which he won't let grow, except for once, before we married. "It's easier this way," he says, whenever I suggest real strands again, "no need to worry about a comb that can break or get lost." Besides, he's had a crew cut since he was a boy. I rub my cheek and mouth against the silk on his chest, around his nipples, and nudge him away from the mirror that looks right back and you don't always know with whose eyes.

"Don't be afraid," Jim pleads in the cabin where we're spending the honeymoon, "Come to me, Ann." I want to but no light, "I find it more intimate," I say, and could the curtains be drawn? Although no other cabin is in view, only the contour of birches, snow, more falling, and our Volkswagen, only I can't say "our" yet; it's Jim's, even though the muffler has been replaced with wedding-gift money. I have trouble with the "our" part of everything, it's all new, like shoes straight from the store you need to wear for a while before they soften up.

I move a little closer, Jim does too. "You're the sexiest person I've ever met," he says. I receive it with a smile but worry that now I need to prove something.

Who took my clothes off? Was it me? Should I not be wearing the fancy nightgown Betty told me to get? Neither blue nor green, with a sash all the way to the floor where it sways when you walk, very cheery. "Come," he says again, "Don't be afraid."

"I'm not," I lie, stiff as a board. So is he, I can see his nakedness against the glow from the fireplace. I bury my face in his neck and count the number of hours before we can run through the snow again as we did all afternoon underneath a sky bluer than I had ever seen and velvet; it was very velvet. This way we went and that way, backward, forward, like a dance or a nursery game. *This is one, I used to sing, This is two, This is three, Dancing makes the legs go free.*

I push myself harder into the licks and nips. He's playful, he's patient. I'm no maven, either, he says, but we'll get it right. He seals my eyes with his mouth.

I kiss him back, chin, chest, wishing it was later, early enough to go to the main building for breakfast, pancakes, lots of syrup, a walk afterward, all bundled up, coat, scarf, mittens, maybe make a snowman. Had no carrot for a nose, no hat, no charcoal for eyes, wouldn't matter; we'd still have fun.

Thud-thud-thud. I stiffen up again. Someone stomping around out there? On the porch already? Convinced of it I press my face deeper into Jim's neck, trying to hide from what'll storm in. Halt! Ears wide open, I keep listening for the door to be kicked in next and the screaming to start. But the noise is gone; those sounds aren't happening anymore. They never were, not even during the war did I hear them. Just the fear of what could've been flaring up.

I was finished with that time, I thought. Had it taken as little as my father's and my stepmother's presence at my wedding to transport me back? The wind must have picked up, that's all it was, plopping snow down the roof onto who knew where or onto what.

We keep on caressing inguino-crural and ilio-inguinal regions, my handbook's way of saying, whatever you can find below the belly and above the knees. I reach further down, all the way back to when I was still wet behind the ears, to the Winterswijk baker who offered a cookie when you bought a loaf of bread, a billy-goat leg if lucky, shaved almonds all around it, chocolate covering each end, you didn't know where to put your teeth first. Playing marbles I liked too, sometimes I came home with four or five more than I had started out with, once a big one even, stripes running across, when you held it up to the light you could see through it as far as the sun. And jumping rope I had a gift for, you could count yourself silly, up to forty and I'd still be at it, only slightly out of breath.

Waiting for what comes next I wonder how much the birch tree still sticks up from the snow, a whole lot probably, an entire yardstick, perhaps, those things are tall, like the poplars in Winterswijk, the same with Usselo, both deep in the past. There was a linden tree there brushing up against my window, made you think it wants to come in, keep me company, leaves and all, heart-shaped and toothed. A few of those leaves I carried with me to America where they dried as I began to sprout. What time is it over there? How close to dawn? Or dark still, as here in the Poconos, far away from everything I know. Finally done thinking, I closed my eyes and put my head on the pillow, right next to this almost-stranger, my husband of a mere night and a half.

IT COULD HAVE BEEN the creaking of a floorboard that woke me or a log shifting its position. I moved a hand around; it was only the mattress. The fire still flickered. Gradually I saw more, I saw him working his way through the cabin. He should turn on the light, would make it easier to find the bathroom. "Jim?" He did find the door, without light, paused but walked on, slowly, step by step, arms held out in front of him. I said his name again, no response, louder then, still no reaction. He kept right on going, toward the outer door now. If he opened that one I'd have to do something, he couldn't go out; it was freezing, and he was naked. He passed it, passed the window too, a handsbreadth away from where the curtain was still closed. The same plank creaked as he approached the grating around the fireplace; the bathroom door again, partly open, the other door, window, armchair, standing exactly where we had left it; and away from there too. His mother used to wander about, didn't she? Just this afternoon he told me, when we were playing in the snow. Suddenly she'd pop up, he said, say nothing, and disappear again. "Intriguing," he called it. It wasn't even far from here, an hour's drive south as well as east from where they had lived for a while. He showed me on the map, and exactly what route we'd take in two days for Detroit, where we'd settle, which Interstate highway, which exit and what road next. "I like to know exactly where I'm going," he explained, "and how I'm going to get there." His mother did her meandering, though, dressed, I assumed, and during the day ...

There he went again, doors, window, chair; stretch of wall, grating. Third time now? Was there a fixed number for something like this? My God, another round coming up. He must be searching for something he suspected was there ...used to be a song game I liked, "Where is Jan? With his nanny-goat cart. He is not here, he is not there, he's off with his girl to America," I'd shout, along with the other kids, not looking yet, first came the counting, "That is four, that is five, that is six."

That was seven...

Would he stop on his own? Or should I do it for him, "C'mon, Jim, back to bed." He might be wanting to do the coupling again, I was still getting over this one. Tomorrow, in a nice way, I'd say something about it, "You seem to have a whole other life at night, did you know that?" Not that there was anything wrong with what he was doing, some people snore in their sleep, others toss and turn, all he did was walk around; it wasn't quite walking, more gliding, a little eerie, actually.

Nervousness, that I hadn't thought of it right away; that's what it was, a sign of nervousness. I'd had a case of it myself, not only tonight, but the evening before the wedding too, double vision so bad I was sure I'd be needing one of those special dogs; diarrhea, nausea, I had it all. I couldn't leave the bathroom and not a thought in my head except "Out." I wanted to get out of it. How could I? My father and step-mother had made the trip just to see me marry, which their local paper had already announced ... what had I started ... I wasn't going through with it. Betty, from the other side of the bathroom door, tried to calm me down. "Let me recapitulate, Annie, what makes a good husband, somebody kind-gentle-cultured-would-make-good-provider pull-no-surprises and who loved his wife probably more than she loved him." It all fit, she thought. "He's even of your faith!"

I watched him emerge from the wall again and begin the cycle all over.

I should wake him up; I ought to. Must. How would some-one react coming out of this sort of trance? He might start screaming, and with no one around but us. Would take cour-age on my part; I was better at doing nothing, at quietly sit-ting in a room marking time, my kind of sleepwalk, hoping for the best, for something unpleasant to end. If ever I had to testify and answer to, *What did it take to get you through the war?* "I tried not to make any waves, your honor," I'd have to say. I'll be more honest yet: "What really got me through was the conviction that before anyone would lay a hand on me, Johan would sacrifice himself."

Still sitting up in bed, I glimpsed Jim passing the chair again. If I were to rouse myself and wake him, wouldn't he get angry—angry, that was the word I couldn't find. I was already afraid he'd be angry when I had left my handbag in some Howard Johnson's ladies room. Everything was in it, even the dictionary I needed. The closer we got to the honeymoon place, the fewer English words traveled along. The money I still owned was in there too, whatever was left after the dress, shoes, veil to match, bouquet, finger sand- wiches for twenty-five guests, and cream puffs and radish roses, rabbi's gratuity, new nightgown, where was it now? My entire capital was in that bag, one hundred dollars—if rounded up—and with Jim having taken a month's advance on his salary to pay for the Poconos, and my job in Detroit not starting for weeks ... when finally I confessed, "I've been forgettish, Jim, bag's away," he was very calm, "Could hap- pen to anyone," he said, and simply turned around, ninety extra miles. He never got angry, I kept checking his face.

It was very silent inside the cabin, no sounds entered my ears, no gusts of wind, no more thuds, only that plank could be heard, whenever Jim's feet brushed across it. And not much showed, some of this I could make out from my bed, some of that, him going by. But only the outline of his face, not what it might express, perhaps what hadn't shown earlier in the day, on our way up. I glanced at the curtain, it wouldn't let the trees through. Neither could I see snow, which had to be there as well, and a new moon perhaps, or about to be, and only a shred of white would squint down. Were there any stars? Surely sky, that would never disap- pear or shrink, only change color ...

I turned my head. The fire still gave off some light, red- dish, like the paper stretched across the rural diorama my sisters had once made inside the shoebox my father's slippers had come in. "Isn't it pretty?" they asked when they gave it to me—"put your eye flush against the hole and tell us what you see"— little animals, tiny trees, little houses, so cozy you'd want to climb right in—if you could. Because of war I had lost the box but not the memory. That still burned.

I AM AWARE of Howard's voice again, I hear it from the edge of the chair I settled on. I don't remember how long ago. It may not even be morning anymore and sunny; it might be pouring, or had that been yesterday's forecast? It's a Wednesday, that I know, and August, of the year I will never forget, 1969.

Soon Howard is bound to finish the eulogy and get to the Dylan Thomas poem I asked him to read, picked from a selection I leafed through, hoping to stumble upon your note. I am sure you know it, Jim, "And Death Shall Have No Dominion." I found it difficult to understand, but with the word "death" in the title I read it many times, trying to draw comfort from someone else's words.

There's so little time left now before you will go one way, forty miles from the city, north, to Ferncliff, where they'll do what I authorized but my mind cannot accept. And I'll be going downtown, back home, where, before I forget, Jim, the phone rang twice this morning. Someone who heard I speak Dutch wanted the translation for "Congratulations." I couldn't answer her; I hung up. And a mother called—we never liked her. How did she know I was already back in New York? Wasn't supposed to be till next week. She invited our girls to the country, to be with her children. When I told her I couldn't concentrate on that right now and why, she said, "Okay, I'll call back tomorrow."

People are crazy, Jim, they don't listen.

Including me; I cast down my eyes.

Yes, you could've said more and exactly what upset you, but I could have insisted on knowing and not ignored all the warning signs. And after you returned, I should have called—I was worried enough. A letter is what I decided on: Make plans for Labor Day; and be sure to have some fun.

Not that it matters, I guess, who failed whom. You're gone and nothing I can think of or do or accuse myself of will bring you back.

"How can you forgive him?" I've been asked. "There's nothing to forgive," I say. "Look where he is. I don't know what he went through; I did not walk his steps." "Sounds noble," I've been told, "but do you mean it?" I hope so. Of course I'll be angry again, and shocked. Each time the phone rings I jump: Another piece of bad news? Or the same, still spooking around in my head? It'll get better, I believe. Am I not still hearing sounds that traumatized me years back? Bad yesterdays tend to hang around and drag along.

You must've thought the world an awful place. In many ways it is, open any day's paper and it stares you in the face. But there are good things in life too.

In Woodstock, at the rock festival, something wonderful happened. You knew about that, I realize, you were still around last week, when all that music and partying turned into impassioned cries of "No More War ..."

I used to ask for "mine" to end, when I was small, after I requested, "Please take care of Sini and me and my father and Rachel, sitting in their rooms, and of my grandmother who has departed on the train," so if anything awful happened, at least I had done what I could.

I never told you, Jim, that I used to pray. There is so much I wish I had said when it was still possible. I'm probably kidding myself again; I'm not comfortable letting someone in that much, something I now see we had in common. And only now can I barely confess to myself how terrified I am of death, and of being near someone who pulls away from life, as my mother did, to whom I used to hold out my arms and came up with nothing. I wish I had been brave enough at least to push those words to the surface. Holding back is a form of lying too.

It's hard not to see myself as co-killer. "You're not," Sini tells me all day long, which makes me feel better—for the space of one second. If only you could tell me. I'm no longer expecting an answer as much as I would like one. I cannot have my way all the time, I know that too; or should. All those privileges I gave myself as though it was an acquired right. *No, Jim, I cannot sleep on your side of the bed, I need to stick out a leg!*

Did I, without mentioning it, have an aura of some-experiences-I-went-through-as-a-kid, whereby anything that upset you must have seemed like nothing? How long can one fall back on the Holocaust? Is that even a fair thing to say, or am I being hard on myself? Of course, it will always be with me. But aren't we all victims of something? You of this, I of that. I shall speak for myself; it has been over for a long time. I should stop hiding behind "my war."

I've never been inside a funeral parlor till this day, Jim, I don't know the rules, but maybe they'll let me leave here before they wheel you away, so I won't have to see. There I go again, trying to spare myself, another habit to shed.

I have to think and talk real fast now—"in closing," Howard just said. But there's a question I must ask; I'll never get this close to you again. When you left Lloyd's and Dottie's apartment and said, "This has been the happiest day of my life," what am I to make of that? It surely is as sad a comment as I ever heard. What does that say about your life with the kids and me? Something else that'll take time to grow into. *Happiest day of your life* ... that those may have been your last words. I need to remember you differently, more whole, more unclouded. Back to when we weren't married. Perhaps to the day you stopped off in Pearl River on your way to Detroit, ostensibly to say good-bye.

You arrived with a plan, to take the Staten Island Ferry, a poor man's version of a trip, you said. But it's a start.

It was late morning when we got to the ferry, and although it was spring, it felt dank. "North Sea weather, Jim, I can taste it." My teeth were chattering, just like now, then as frightened of losing you as of ending up with you. We stood by the railing, your arms around me, tight, like a swimming vest. That's how we passed the Statue of Liberty that I had not seen since I arrived in America and mistook it for Jesus. Water we discussed, you did, how the sun sets on it and the moon silvers its darkness, it could guide you to as far away as Japan and beyond. Why Japan? You didn't know. It might have to do with the picture that was always up on a wall ever since you were a little boy, a seascape. You used to pretend you too were on a voyage, but not letting on, your mother might pull you back from the rowboat you dreamed this in, where each day you hoped that it was Friday and Bob would come and visit. The boat was dilapidated, it never left the bit of grass along your house at Lock No. 12, the Delaware River very close.

The boat I'm seeing now would not sink, you've made sure of that. It is watertight and can take you anywhere. I imagine you have scooped up a handful of rays, sun, moon, all of it, to light your way for the voyage across bays and rivers and oceans you used to make up names for. I see one body of water after another unrolling before you—waves churning and rising into mountains.

Jim would keep going forward—I can't help but know that now, when time differences cease to exist, with only one thing on his mind, as he must have had that night just a few days ago, when he broke loose from his past and journeyed off for real. All burdens gone at last.

"And death shall have no dominion," Howard repeats.

With Sini's hand on mine, I listen. "I hear it all, sky, sea, land, lovers lost. But that death shall have no dominion." He makes it sound very beautiful, as if nothing ends and every-thing goes and comes back, rising and falling like the tides of a sea. As the words sink in and I begin to feel what they mean, that death is only part of the story, that it neither erases the person nor the love there was, my voice wells up, if only inward still, *"Requiem aeternam,"* Grant them eter-nal rest, as my choir used to sing, and I faded out, throat locked. Now my lips are moving, part of a Hebrew prayer for the dead is coming back, *Yisgadal v'yiskadash*, the first language of mourning ever to enter my ears.

Over the years I've meant to tell my children the truth about their father's death. It never seemed to be a good time. When I did, they were just about to strike out on their own.

"You ruined my dream," Julie shouted, that someday he'd be back.

I bent my head, wondering what she meant.

"How could he have done that?" she shouted next. Did she remember wrong? Hadn't he taken them on outings? To the movies, *Mary Poppins* and the Beatles one. Hadn't he read to them? Sung to them? Was that not true, either?

"It's the same Daddy," Kathy answered, her arms around her younger sister. "It all did happen. Only now we know."

"Shall I tell you how?" I asked. *Please don't,* they said.

They left then, to spend the evening together. I went to Central Park, to an outdoor concert, convinced they were denouncing me, for both the lie as well as the truth.

What piece of music moved me to suddenly sit up? Was I seeing things? Kathy and Julie were walking over. How had they found me among the tens of thousands of people crammed onto towels and sheets? "We had no trouble," they said. "As if you were a magnet that pulled us straight to you."

I lay down again, holding them tight, and gave thanks to whatever deity cared to hear. I still had so much to be grateful for.

Acknowledgements

There are many people I need to thank. Let me make it short and single out only a few:

Micki McCabe, who would have killed me had I not written this book; Sal Robinson, who found Melville House for me; Tsipi Kelller, an early reader, who was very encouraging ("Keep at it, darling"); Pamela Manche Pearce with a worldly sense that outmatches mine; and last, but surely not least, my daughters Kathy and Julie, who, in spite of the fact that having this book published is not easy for them, have never failed in their loving support.